This book is the second in the 'Courier' series which show how campsite couriers are beset by the weird demands of clients and how they retaliate without informing Head Office of their machinations.

The innocuous reports show the substance but the text shows the subversive strategies which the couriers employ to counter the onslaught of demanding clients.

These books are based on the author's personal experiences whilst working on campsites in Brittany and are fine examples of the 'us versus them' attitudes of people when faced with a little authority.

The title is an invitation to the reader to participate. The book should be digested and the reader then complete the title with his own assessment. Should it be: A Courier's Reports are Never accurate, or believable, candid, devious, erudite, fabricated, gibberish, honest, incredible, judgemental, kind, ludicrous, etc, etc..to zealous.

Whatever you decide it should not be: A Courier's Work is Never Read.

ABOUT THE AUTHOR

Facts about the author are unchanged from the description in his previous book, 'A Courier's Work is Never...'. He was born in the same place, worked as before and his life followed the same pattern much as one would expect.

Peter Goodlad

A Courier's Reports are Never....

Published by Amazon

In association with CasaBlanca

Although I must thank the wits and half-wits, called clients by the Camping Firms, who unwittingly supplied me with the characters and situations portrayed, I hereby --

Dedicate this book to my friends, Matt and Mel without whose unstinting help and encouragement it would never have been published and, of course, to the long-suffering Sandy for her tolerance and support.

Chapter 1

The black Mercedes van roared at us like an avenging demon, it's trailer bounced on screaming springs, dust jetted from beneath tortured tyres and the crashing of contents orchestrated it's fury. "Mon dieu," cried Hervé, and took to flight.

It was our first introduction to Dan the maintenance man. And our first intimation of violently flowing undercurrents.

Our second season as couriers had started in the same gentle manner as the first, once again lulling us with false serenity.

Sandy and I arrived, out of season, at Dole du Mire Chateau Camping for the refresher course. Before the hordes of screaming clients descended, all was tranquillity and light.

The sun shone as we drove our camper van through the entrance. The camp's owner paused from contemplating the freshly revived grass on his manicured golf course and addressed us with courtesy.

"Monsieur, madam. I regret that the campsite is not officially open."

"We're couriers," I explained, "Smartcamp's finest."

It says much for aristocratic breeding that the Count's demeanour underwent no change. A slight twitch of an eyebrow, a minimal tremor throughout the body, were the only outward indications of the suffering that couriers of previous years had inflicted upon his person and property. Stories of drunken couriers dropping tureens of scalding curry over him, driving a tractor into his Rolls, sinking the boats on his lake and setting fire to the bar stirred in our minds but remained unspoken. In the distance the gleaming new bar sat, as a mute memorial to mayhem past, like a Phoenix upon the ashes of the old.

"Ah," replied the Count des Awks. His ungrudging acceptance of us was perhaps because, being older, we were obviously past the first rash of youth. Or it may have been that, over the centuries, suffering had become an accepted way of life and his family had been subjected to greater indignities than couriers could perpetrate. It was said that, on Bastille Day, his mother ignored the bourgeois revellers carousing around, wore mourning, and lit candles for the poor souls of her breed who had lost their heads in the Revolution.

"Reception", said the current Count, "is beyond the lake", his body gave an involuntary spasm, "behind the new bar?"

- O -

The training course was a repetition of the previous year's.

Michael, Smartcamp's M D, explained how we couriers would be all things to all

A Courier's Reports are Never...

men. Guides, nannies, helpmates, friends, wet nurses, doormats, translators, cleaners, footballs, and all round jolly good eggs. And throughout we would conduct ourselves in an intelligent, kind, helpful, courteous and sober manner, "in the way your predecessors have carried out their duties and given the impeccable service our clients have come to expect", he enlarged, fingers crossed and lying through his teeth.

Other superior beings from the permanent staff at Head Office came to explain to us lowly, temporary couriers the intricacies of the work.

Hubert Briggs, our link man at headquarters, proudly displayed a box of tools, personally designed by himself, which would enable us to carry out any repairs with the exception of those to clients for which we would be issued a first aid kit. "It will cater for all your needs", he said, snapping down the lid and wincing, "much thought and research has gone into it?"

Work beyond our capabilities would, he explained, sucking his thumb, be carried out by Jonah, our roving Maintenance Officer, who could be contacted via himself and the stores in Central France could be phoned direct for replacement items. He told us how Smartcamp and other similar, but inferior firms, rented plots from site owners and placed upon then tents or mobile homes which couriers were expected to service and clean. Also we were thoroughly to familiarise ourselves with the part of France in which we would be unleashed so that we could advise clients as to the best restaurants, the most picturesque countryside and the most attractive towns to visit.

As the other trainee couriers were school-leavers without transport who would be paid £80 per week, the way to perform these impossible tasks was not explained. As a meal with wine in a good restaurant could cost £40 a head and taxis were expensive, the only method open to the bemused courier was to duck out of the eatery without paying then, satiated with good food and wine, steal a car and tootle around the neighbourhood. But this was counterproductive as, according to the contract thrust under our noses, misdemeanours would merit dismissal. Any infringement of the courier code would bring stern retribution. Even the courier who burnt down the bar had been fired.

We were shown how to welcome clients and bid them farewell. How to treat and cherish them. Issue them with goodies and games from our treasure chest. Revive them from fainting spells and extinguish them if they combusted. Fire precautions seemed to be uppermost in our mentor's minds.

Uppermost in Cynthia's mind was how to enchant the client's kiddies. She was an ex-childrens' courier now promoted to "Head Office Person Charged With Beguiling Client's Issue." A sort of absentee Pied Piper. She sat in England sending fond cooing directives at us poor suckers in the firing line who had to care for the brats.

A big selling point in Smartcamp's doctrine was that they had a children's club which would take the loathsome creatures off the hands of suffering parents. It was, for the parents, the main attraction of this type of holiday and we were the mugs, who had to entertain their awful offspring.

I didn't mention this to the other couriers on the course; I'd had to find out the hard way.

Cynthia had a nauseating affection for the kids and singled us out. "We had letters about you and Sandy. Parents said how happy they were with the way you organised the club and entertained the children."

The other couriers eyed us with respect. I didn't explain that, adjacent to the campsite, I discovered an assault course. We used to run the swine round it and return them after 2 hours, knackered, to their mums and dads. The exhausted offspring were therefore too finished to give their parents the hard time they were used to and the result was semi-comatose kids and a good time had by all. No wonder they liked us.

I looked round at these eager faced youngsters. Newly tossed into the sea of life they had no knowledge of what awaited them and were unaware that they had been cast into the deep end. It was alright for Sandy and myself. At our age we had been pounded by the vicissitudes of life and were still afloat. I wondered how many of these couriers would survive the season and the battering by clients.

I wished them well.

- O -

The three day course to turn us into dependable know-alls bumbled on through the balmy days of late April, lulling the unwary into a false sense of wellbeing. Relaxed in the classroom, lethargic in the sun-flecked outdoors, or gently noshing in the restaurant, we received no hint of the hectic buffeting which was the on-site courier's lot.

Zoë, the new Brittany supervisor, gave us scenarios to act out. One of us took the part of a courier, another a client, others were client's wives, friends, site owners, or sewerage supervisors. Usually the scene was an irate client being placated by a chirpy courier about the smell, or the view, or the showers being cold. Our colleague's interpretations were of mildly irritated clients easily pacified by ineffectual platitudes. They had no notion of screaming banshees demanding instant rectification of the stench, or of marauding husbands seeking a punch bag to relieve the frustration of a hectoring wife. I could have dropped this bombshell on them and had them scattering for cover. That is, if they believed me. But I refrained as I doubt that they would have credited my account, experience being the best, albeit the most traumatic, teacher.

The course, like a watered down curry, wended its way mildly to the end. The next step was the painful one of montage. i.e. the dash around various sites erecting heavy tents and equipping them, scouring out last season's detritus from mobiles and slaving for 12 hours each day at manual labour. It was not something we relished but it was a move nearer to our summer domicile in the Dordogne. I mentioned this to Zoë.

"Dordogne?" she said, looking puzzled, "why the Dordogne?"

I pointed out that Jane, last year's Brittany manager, had told us that, as seasoned couriers willing to submit ourselves into bondage for a second time, we would be allowed to select the area we wanted. "Dordogne appeals to us," I said complacently, "I put it on the application form."

"And where it said, 'position applied for', you put, managing director."

"Well, one never knows?" I said airily.

"We do." she replied. "You're working for me in Brittany".

The sharp pain in my ankle was caused by Sandy hacking my shin.

When I stopped hopping about, Zoë asked, "Did you find the course instructive?"

"We learnt all this last year. All we need to know is how to put up these new mini-tents for kids."

"Can't show you." she said, "They haven't come through yet from the manufacturers".

I hoped this display of delayed efficiency wasn't a foretaste of the season.

Fortunately, the heavy graft and toil of montage was denied us this year.

Whether Zoë was contrite about not making me managing director, or trying to show that working for her in Brittany was preferable to being in the Dordogne, she eased our path by temporarily allocating us to a site at St. Cast, in Northern Brittany, as caretakers charged with preparing tents and mobiles.

A beautiful site overlooking a bay from which we gleaned fresh mussels, the owner was a friendly Frenchman, the manager his efficient, agreeable daughter. The nearby town had a pretty harbour and attractive pedestrian precinct. We could have settled happily there but the small number of units made it a one courier site. So after nine days we moved back to Dole where we serviced tents erected in our absence. And, after five days there, we drove to St. Armand Camping at Fougenant, on the coast south of Corentin the ancient capital of Brittany, which we were to enhance with our presence for the summer.

And where we met Dan, the maintenance man.

- O -

He wasn't our maintenance man; he worked for the rival firm of Mucus (Marvellous) Holidays, a firm privately owned by Marvin Mucus and his family, a small company on about a dozen different sites. Dan was also their area manager, trouble shooter, supervisor, electrician, plumber, stores organiser, relief courier, and complaints department. He also had his own problems.

"Mon dieu", shouted Hervé, and left my side as though fired from a rusty musket.

Fortunately the van and I bounced in opposite directions as it tore past after the fleeing Hervé. A few minutes of revving around the site, then it returned.

"Missed the bastard", said Dan, alighting.

I took in the suffused features between the black beard and the wild black hair. "You don't like him", I guessed.

"Why should I", said Dan.

I cast my thoughts back to Hervé and looked for attributes that could attract such violent dislike. Tall, thin, and smelly due to a life spent toiling in cesspits, manholes and drains, he had a flared nose and deep creases bracketing the misshapen mouth which results from distorting it to speak French. However he was friendly and helpful to a fault, and although I would not want, to be closeted with him in a confined space, I saw no reason for wiping him out.

But your courteous courier does not probe on first meeting; so I said I was Pete and he said he was Dan and we cordially shook hands.

Having introduced ourselves and our respective positions in the scheme of life we became chummy and chatted of this and that; although I forbear to query the homicidal side of his nature that I had witnessed. Instead I commented on his van.

"Come and look", he said, sliding back the side door with a horny hand.

The van was as diverse as his job indicated. Behind the driving cab were living quarters fully equipped with seating, table, bed, wardrobe, sink and cooker. Double external doors at the rear gave access to racks of plumbing and electrical fittings, screws, nuts and bolts, and fixed to the doors were sets of tools. His trailer contained spares and equipment from gas heaters to cups and saucepans. The unit was transport, home, office, stores and workshop. It had everything the working man could wish for. I told him so.

"Except a wife," he replied; enigmatically, I thought, but before I could question further he pushed off to maintain something.

And I pottered off to assist the montage mob.

- O -

This montage mob had been seconded from the site at Benemaas. It consisted of the scrag end of the touring team that had roved throughout Brittany heaving tents into position and filling them with equipment. At each site the relevant couriers had been

7

dropped off until all that was left were the ones considered of insufficient standard to service a site. These were placed on large sites where their ineffectual or incompetent attributes would be merged into the mass and show up only as minor hiccups in the working body. As a temporary inconvenience we had inherited these unwanted souls to assist.

Bev was a workshy redhead enamoured of Jim, the scrawny one with a tic. Jenny, the blonde sexpot, was worried about her nails which were showing signs of recovery after a nervous winter as a waitress. Monica was used to mummy waiting or her and Ben had been pushed into the job to help build his weak physique and weaker character. Paul was a hardworking, steady pleasant lad with a clean driving licence and a clear cut, handsome face. We suspected that he had been handpicked by Zoë as relief driver and for her general relief. He was willing but easily exhausted.

With these beguiling assistants we put up tents and doled out equipment but even with careful supervision things went wrong.

Even though I removed stones from tent floors before ground sheets went down, they managed to get tree roots, thorny branches and bricks under them so that, during the season, clients would stub their toes, or erupt howling, clutching their feet. Bev managed to force large mattresses into small mattress covers and the resulting bed resembled a hard undulating corrugated iron sheet. Jenny tended to hang ceilings upside down, leaving an enthralling, 'this side up' pattern on the underside. Ben and Paul were busy vying for the easy job of driving the van; a contest usually won by Paul as Zoë was saving his energy for the evening.

All in all it was nerve wracking and we were glad when they left so that we could get down to putting things right.

"There," said Zoe. "that's given you a good start, and she drove her slobs off to handicap the senior courier at Benemaas.

CHAPTER 2

"Jean-Claud will deal with that," said Madam S, the camp owner, indicating a retarded looking, stocky Frenchman of about 25 who was trimming the hedge. He had springy curly hair coating a head that lacked the back bit, a hooked nose and square jaw and, from the side, he resembled a teapot. At the sound of his name he looked round and dropped his jaw in an inane grin. Had Madam been English she would have added, "you can't get the help, you know," but instead, feeling she had left us in good hands, she trotted her small body off on thin but efficient legs.

"It's Europlug," said Jean-Claud, "you need an adaptor. "Hervé, the odd-job man, knows the electrics, he will help,"

A Courier's Reports are Never...

And so saying he ambled off to greet a transporter that was delivering two new mobiles leaving the hedge half trimmed. We later discovered the Jean-Claud was the world's greatest half-finisher. All the jobs he started were abandoned at mid-completion, in much the same way that his maker had left his mind, and I spent the rest of the season remembering him as I watched the unbalanced sprout of his hedge.

We were now well into commissioning our units. We had adjusted the tight pegging of the tents so that the zip doors would close, had replaced mattress covers, reassembled kitchen units, re-hung ceilings and re-fixed groundsheets. Had re-arranged equipment in tents and mobiles so that it complied with inventory sheets. Everything was well in hand except for odd items missed from the installation of our new mobiles by Fred, Smartcamp's services expert.

He was busy fixing mobiles when we first arrived. His wife was sprawled with a wrench beneath one and her daughter worked on the electrical terminal with an old chisel. He regarded me morosely over a cup of tea.

"Nice to see you again, Fred", I said convivially. "Still on the old maintenance racket?"

"Naw," he replied, "I bin promoted. Only do installations now don't piss about with maintenance. Nerve wrecking that was all them odd jobs. Now I just come in, bang, bang, fix it all together and that's it finished." He took a swig of tea and settled deeper into his camp chair. "All completed in one operation and then on to the next site. Hard work but, satisfying. Want a cup "o tea?"

Sandy and I said yes please, one for each if he could manage it. "No problem," he replied, kicking his wife's leg. "Hoy, get Pete and Sandy some tea."

He regarded us mournfully as Hoy crawled out and poured tea.

"Got a problem you have," he pointed at a yawning gap between the lounge floor and the ground. "They only delivered two-tread, steps and you need three tread. Better order some from stores."

"Right," I said.

"Oh, and there's no site electrics to three mobiles. Can't connect it till it's there. Better see Hervé."

"Right." I said.

"And there's no water to four mobiles. I left the pipes uncoupled. Need's turning on somewhere".

"See Hervé?" I said.

"Right," said Fred, "soon as you can. When's your first clients?"

"Saturday."

A Courier's Reports are Never...

"Today's Monday. You better phone stores now." Fred was on expert on delegation.

Later he drove his family workforce up to me at the phone box by the camp entrance.

"Steps will be here by tomorrow lunchtime." I told him.

He took out his pipe, coughed. "Better phone Briggs; get Jonah here to fix them."

"But," I pointed out, "that's part of installation."

"Not once I've gone, it's not. Then it falls under maintenance."

He put the van into gear. "Remind him to connect water to those four and electrics to the other three."

As he drove off I went to phone Briggs and pondered on Fred.

Delegation was his forté. But he took it to extremes.

Jean - Claud did everything by half

-oops

- O -

And so the week spun on, each day following the preceding in predictable, but rapid progression. Time definitely flew as we hurtled about from early morn until late evening and Saturday's deadline loomed.

It was the same for couriers of the other firms.

Only two firms apart from Smartcamp on this site.

Mucus' units were being commissioned by Dan and an unshaven hairy primitive on loan from a site in the Dordogne. Usually he was in the hills near Sarlat, noted as being the cradle of civilisation, and must have given clients an idea of what pre-cultural man was like before they feasted their eyes on more advanced cave drawings. He shambled

A Courier's Reports are Never...

about on Dan's directives, dragging lengths of drain pipe or carrying concrete blocks, but looked very out of place next to machinery.

The other firm, Heavenly Holidays, was represented by two couriers wearing blue track suit trousers with "Heavenly" inscribed in white on blue T shirts amongst tastefully embroidered clouds. She, small blonde and very pretty, he, medium height, with good shoulders and excellent features which were spoiled by a tight, scowl. Both ran about with equipment, raising little spurts of dust as they dashed, faces drawn in frantic concentration. We tried to speak to them but he avoided our pre-chat glance and turned away scowling. She was more responsive and blinked before looking away.

"It's all this work," I said, "they'll be more relaxed when it's over,"

"What will they be like in high season," replied Sandy, "if they can't speak to people now."

"Reminds me, I must speak to Briggs; find out where Jonah's got to."

It was friday morning. The three-tread steps had arrived from stores with other oddments on tuesday but no word no had been heard of our errant maintenance man.

On the way to the phone I passed Jean-Claud hitching a newly delivered mobile to his tractor. He had positioned ours before we arrived and was now completing the placing of Heavenly's, which were easily recognisable being in two shades of blue enhanced by white clouds with cherubs perched on them.

He grinned and waived happily. He loved driving the camp's machinery of which there was a plethora; three various sized tractors, one with a hoist for rubbish containers, an excavator, a dumper truck, van, lorry, motor mower complete with idiot sized seat, and, when not playing with these, he dashed around in a four wheel drive vehicle with 'passion' inscribed on the spare wheel cover. He seemed to have redundant legs.

Madam S of the unpronounceable surname was gracing the steps of reception with her worried thin body as I passed. "Peter," she called.

"Madam," I replied, "ca va?"

"Well at the moment." She smiled demurely and tapped a notice, "will you let your clients have a translation of these camp rules? They must conform with them implicitly."

"I will post them on my notice board." I said referring to the Smartcamp board which gave the couriers' names, places of interest, and times of opening for banks and shops and loads of other fascinating information which was ignored en bloc by our clients. They preferred to ask as they either liked the personal touch or enjoyed wasting our time. Or, perhaps, being avid newspaper readers, they no longer believed the written word.

I hoped that this site would not enforce stringent regulations as had our site of last year where clients had been harried and hounded by a power-crazed manager. But looking at the kindly Madam S blinking through her wire frames I doubted it, although one can never go totally by appearances. I used to have a small gracious grandmother who was a complete martinet.

"Madam," I said, testing her flexibility, "the gymnasium is never unlocked before ten whereas the only free time I have in which to train is between seven and eight in the morning. Could it be opened earlier?"

She nodded affably. "Ask Jean-Claud. He will give you a key."

This site was too good to be true but, before I could thank her, a grinding crash impinged on the conversation. She startled like an owl hearing it's barn being bashed.

"Ho, ho," I chortled, knowing it was not one of our mobiles, "it's young Half-done at it again."

She shot me an unfathomable glance before sprinting off towards the source of the sound. My guffaw was perhaps ill-timed as Halfsharp had probably belted the mobile into some of her property. However that was their problem. Briggs gave his response to mine.

"I remember you phoned me" he said thoughtfully, "but wasn't sure if it was serious."

"You promised to get Jonah here."

"Did I? I wonder where he is. Do you really need him?"

I made a gnashing noise down the phone.

"Bad line this," he continued, "just fixing some steps was it?"

"And four without water and three without electrics."

"Not so bad then, eh?"

"Seven out of ten out of commission and no steps fitted to any."

"Yes, I see your point. Clients arriving tomorrow, eh? For how many units?"

"Five mobiles and two tents."

"Tents don't need steps." he pointed out reasonably.

I made that gnashing noise again.

"Right," he decided, "I'll try to get Jonah. You don't know where he is, I suppose?"

I told him "no" and sadly replaced the phone.

All our commissioning was finished apart from reception and the children's club tent. I completed our notice boards by placing a picture of a psychedelically painted erotic dancer in an impossibly contorted position above Sandy's name and a dignified photo of Dirk Bogard wearing a moustache and an expression of bland innocence above mine. Then I, with due poetic licence, translated the camp rules as I doubted that Madam S would read beyond the heading. Next, I read the computer sheets again and checked them with my programme.

We had to complete the bar-chart programme from the computer advice supplied by head office and take cognisance of clients' wishes – whether they wanted to be next to a friend, or have a shady or sunny site, or not be near the bar, or have us run over and fan them every twenty minutes – then place them into their temporary homes and hope that they were satisfied with their lot.

As far as possible I tried to group together people with kids of a similar age and put people with babies on the fringe so that their howling would keep clients of other companies awake rather than ours. The only thing a tent wall will exclude, to a degree, is sight and smell although they sometimes do transmit shadows and stench.

Our programme showed that we would have thirteen units filled by the second day and all the rest by Wednesday. With ten tents and ten mobiles occupied by 42 adults and 30 children the following day, Thursday, would be a good time to hold an aperitif party and catch the suckers before they mingled on their own cognisance.

We had, Head Office decreed, to hold some form of get-together each week if feasible, for which we could charge our clients a reasonable amount. This was to engender a community of spirit, and make the punters feel wanted and part of the Smartcamp family, thus ensuring loyalty and that they would travel with us again. We were abetted in flogging tickets by the average Englishman's need to be introduced before making friends. We had noted, last year, that they would sit mutely outside their tents within spitting distance of each other with only a stilted 'good morning' to carry them through the day. But after a party introduction they would gather in groups shouting, bellowing with laughter, having a good time, and generally ruining the tranquillity for everyone else, which is what a holiday is all about.

But we first had to get the mobiles fixed.

- O -

Saturday came but Jonah didn't. Unless he was coming somewhere else.

When we had purchased some plants to grace the front of reception, we noticed that the garden centre also sold nuts, bolts and electrical fittings, so I dashed off and bought all necessary bits and pieces and spent the morning fixing steps, plumbing water pipes and connecting electrics. All with my own tools from the camper as the Briggs Wonder box failed to materialise, much like the promised Jonah.

Everything worked except the power in one mobile. Hervé had fixed up the site

14

supply but this one mobile baffled us. Eventually he fetched his tester, checked the electrics, found the fault, and replaced the circuit breaker. All was now in order and his help was far in excess of the call of duty. The mobile was my problem, not his. I really couldn't see why anyone, even Dan, didn't like him. I mentioned this.

He shrugged. " A strange man" he opinioned, "he is not, ow you say, tolerant.

Not knowing Dan, apart from the odd chat and watching him on a Hervé hunt, I refrained from further comment. Instead, I handed Hervé a bottle of wine, thanked him and shook his hand. The French like that.

He licked his lips, smacked them, and took himself off to open the bottle. The French are like that.

And thus, having commissioned everything in sight, except, Halfdone, I settled down to await the first client.

CAMPSITE RULES

1. Avoid excessive noise and games that disturb others, e.g. bagpipe playing, wife beating, choral singing and formula racing.

2. Be silent between 10p.m. and 7a.m.; snore quietly.

3. Speed limit on site is 10 kpm except in reverse gear.

4. Any car driving on site between 10p.m. and 7a.m. must have the engine removed.

5. Park on own site and not on other people.

6. Be tidy and hygienic. Do not litter the site with old wrappers, soiled underwear, discarded wives, and other rubbish.

7. Rubbish must be placed in bins and not in neighbouring tents. Excrete into the appropriate receptacle.

8. Do not festoon the site with washing; we are not interested in the condition of your garments.

9. Deceased campers must not be deposited in the burial mound which is exclusively for Neanderthals and suchlike minority groups.

10. Do not cut flowers, shrubs, trees or fellow campers or knock nails in them.

11. Do not have open fires, take care with barbecues; anyone burning down the site will have to pay for it.

12. There is a first aid kit in reception and your couriers will give the kiss of life to attractive clients.

13. Do not smoke in the pool as the water puts cigarettes out.

14. No glasses, bottles, aqualungs, submarines, dogs, balls, gum, lilos, yoyos, or speedboats allowed in the pool.

15. All campers must conform with police formalities including body search, fingerprinting, victimisation, brutality and malicious prosecution.

16. The management is not responsible for theft, so someone else must have done it.

CHAPTER 3

This year, knowing what to expect, we were not so apprehensive.

Also, on the course, they had played down the savage, vicious side of clients and spoke of them as smiling, genial philanthropists, not as sullen paranoiac misanthropists as some we had encountered. And so we placidly waited, brimming with sanguinity, determined to take things as they came, anticipating nothing.

Being within striking distance of the channel ports we could, with reasonable accuracy, predict client's times of arrival. Unless of course they were unable to map read, navigate, follow instructions or think logically; states which covered 90% of our inmates.

If however they stuck to the laid down route as written in our guide with clever little illustrations, they had a reasonable chance of arriving before the end of their holiday.

We had estimated that our first arrival, Mr. Robins, could be with us by 1 p.m. At 1.05 to our surprise he rolled up.

More surprises — he was genial, friendly, relaxed and smiling, and his family was cheerful and happy. Usually we received a car load of snarling, fighting primitives fraught from the journey and each other's company. But here was this jolly fat chap with his hearty overweight family, the only unpleasant note struck, apart from a sudden shower, was his first words.

"When's children's club?" he said.

I thought quickly, determined to have it as late as possible, but another heavy influx was due on Wednesday.

Best to start gradually with small numbers. "Tuesday." I replied.

"Goody, goody." chirped his fat son and larger fat daughter, "Will

we get stickers?"

They were alluding to a bunch of pictures of the Smartcamp Bear showing him in unnatural poses such as washing up, shopping or helping mummy do the housework. None showing him belting baby sister, throwing tantrums, breaking windows, or other normal healthy pursuits. It was another instance of Cynthia's lack of child knowledge; she had never been a mother.

"You get stickers if you're good," I said, quelling exuberance at the outset. "I will question your parents later."

And leaving them apprehensive and thoughtful I showed the family up gleaming, but shaky, steps into their brand new mobile.

17

A Courier's Reports are Never...

- O -

Our next arrival, Mr. Philpot, showed up two hours late.

"Your maps wrong," he muttered in a sneaky manner. "1`ll inform your office of this."

"Yes, of course, please do." I smarmed, knowing these useless navigational misfits always blamed something else.

"And when's children's club?" He snapped.

He had a baby, too young for the club, and an innocent looking daughter. "Tuesday," I said.

"What! Not until then?"

Only another two days but his reaction was too violent. I took another look at the daughter but she looked blandly back.

"It's not long to wait, dear," said his smart red-coiffured wife, sadly in the manner of one who's child is about to be sacrificed. It made me wonder how they viewed us as I shovelled them into their mobile.

And turning away, l bumped into this little fat bloke.

- O -

"Smartcamp?" he said.

Considering I was wearing this year's orange, red, green and purple uniform with 'Smartcamp' wording smeared on it back and front, his perspicacity took me by surprise. "How did you know I asked?"

"Smartcamp," he repeated, thumping himself on the chest.

I wondered what dumb client they had landed me with this time. About 24 years old; projecting above the T shirt cloaking a pear shaped body was a pear shaped head surmounted by vertical hair which should have made him look taller. It didn't.

I tried to remember who should arrive next. "Panter," I said. He looked puzzled. I tried again.

"Me, Smartcamp," I said, tapping my chest, then pointed at him, "who you?"

"Me? Smartcamp." he replied.

"Let us go to reception," I said tiredly, "and sort this out." Perhaps the sight of his name on our programme would jog his memory.

"Why?" he sounded surprised. "I'm Smartcamp. Jonah, the Maintenance Officer."

Sadly I wondered if this was a foretaste of our future relationship. "You're a bit late. I've done the work."

"Late? Yes, I suppose I am. I had a problem with the van."

I wondered what problem could make him five days late. "what was it?" I asked.

"Loose lead on the distributor, but the garage soon fixed it."

He sounded like the ultimate in maintenance men.

"Got here as soon as I could," he continued, "only got the message from Briggsey last night."

Oh, good. All I needed were excuses.

"The works all done. I fixed the steps."

He trod gingerly on a step, tried another. "Not very firm."

"Tighten them up." I said. He bounced up and down, gave his verdict, "actually I think they'll hold."

"Would you also care to thoroughly test the water and electrics?"

"Might as well have a quick look while I'm here." he said, strolling off the wrong way and filling me with confidence.

- O -

On the way back I ran into Elulia the toilet cleaning lady who, together with Hervé, inhabited a beat-up mobile next to the workshops.

"Good afternoon." I said politely.

She regarded me blankly then reached up into her nest of curly hair. There was a click as she switched off a hidden walkman. "What?" she responded.

"What's a nice girl like you doing in a place like this?" I asked.

"Cleaning shithouses." she said.

She was English. About 50, wearing jeans, dark sweater, a bucket and mop, she was one of the remnants of the "Flower Power People." Wandering around Europe after the demise of the San Francisco flower cult, she found herself ill equipped to earn a living and had resorted to womanual labour. And, feeling at a loose end when Hervé was busy dogs-bodying she took on the site job of Sanitation and Ablution Purification Officer; as Smartcamp might put it in order to boost the prestige and thereby lower the wages.

So we passed the time of day in idle chat while I tried to determine from her the attitude of the camp owners and find out where they had dug their pitfalls.

19

"Madam Sin," she replied, "isn't bad but tends to panic."

"A French characteristic." I opinioned.

"Well, yes," she responded thoughtfully, "it is, isn't it?"

Having close contact with the emotional side of Hervé she would know all about panic, particularly as generated by a vindictive Dan.

But before I could question on the reason for that panic/hate relationship she pressed on.

"Mind you madam Sin only bought the campsite last July. She worked together with the previous people for the rest of the season, so it's difficult to say what's she's really like"

"She must be pretty tolerant to employ young Half-done." I said.

"Who?"

"That moronic creature," I dredged my memory for his name."Jean Claud.

"Oh, he's a real arsehole." she said, and I bowed to her superior knowledge in this sphere. With her job she would have an intimate grasp of the ablutive side of peoples' natures.

"Its hilarious," I chuckled, "to see him crunching mobiles into gateposts and things." I held my sides. "Ho, ho. You should have seen Madam S's face when he bent the last one. She showed genuine eighteen carrot panic."

"You're very easy-going," she said, regarding me interestedly, "considering the way he mangled yours."

I emitted a strangled gulp.

"Trees," she said, "he banged them on trees. Dan won't let him touch his."

And, without bothering to ask why Dan wanted to touch. Hervé, I galloped off for a close look at our own mutilation.

- O -

"They're not so bad," said Jason, complaisantly chewing on a piece of mutton, "they'll be all right."

"But there's a hole right through one" I protested.

"Only as far as the polystyrene insulation."

"But the water will get in."

He filled his mouth with saffroned rice. Yellow spread round his pink lips and he

A Courier's Reports are Never...

looked as though he was peering over a daffodil.

"Not if you cover it with polysulphide sealant."

"Me?" I said, "but you're the maintenance man.

"Officer," he corrected. "I do the big jobs. Small stuff I advise on. Couriers do the running repairs."

He must have taken Fred's correspondence course in delegation.

"There are gouges on two others and three have bent useless gutters." I pointed out.

"Nothing detrimental," he said, "and rain is bound to run off the roof anyway." He took another mouthful, "that's because of gravity," he muttered indistinctly, getting technical, 'pass the chutney."

We were sitting outside our courier tent relishing both the warm evening following the afternoon showers, and Sandy's curry.   Jonah had been hovering around like a little fat blowfly until Sandy, unable to swat him away, had stretched our evening meal to feed three. Or feed four if you counted the way he noshed.

"Two of the sink traps leak," I said.

He took another plateful of curry. "Just needs a spanner on them."

"I didn't get a toolbox from stores"

"We did. Lovely things they are. All three of us maintenance officers took one. And the van drivers. Worth having, they are."

"We would like one."

"No chance," he said, digging into the mango chutney, "Briggsy only ordered enough for the sites to have one each. You were the last site serviced and there weren't enough to go round."

"Mind you," he said comfortingly, "you're not the only site that missed out."

It was a prime example of how organisation topples with the advance of avarice.

"I've no tool box," I said cunningly, "I'll have to use yours."

"Forgot to bring it," he said promptly, "go and buy some tools from the supermarket."

I was thwarted of comment on Jonah's generosity by the advent of a young chap who had been hanging around us much as Jonah had been hanging around the embryo curry.

"Smartcamp?" He asked, nervously.

"The one and only." I replied courteously, pushing my plate away. It was immediately fielded by Jonah.

Sandy had been stuffing the punters down their lairs for most of the afternoon. Now it was my turn.

"Mr. Panter?" I asked, and took him off to reception away from the sound of Jonah slurping.

- O -

"There's something wrong with your map," said Mr. Panter, "we've been lost for hours."

I looked into his twenty year old face and put it down to inexperience. Probably trying to excuse his ineptitude in front, of his friend and their young wives.

"Quite," I murmured, "we do it on purpose to test your initiative."

In order to orientate him and prevent his driving into the estuary, I indicated the swimming pool and bar but forbear to mention the not-yet-open restaurant and shop.

"The site, as you can see," I explained, "is steeply sloping down to the estuary and therefore levelled into terraces. Your mobile is on the third terrace up with a beautiful view through the trees. If you drive down there, turn sharp left by the tree with 28 on it and fork right, after fifty yards, I will cut through the centre and meet, you at your

mobile. Number eight." I added for good measure.

He looked at me through travel-weary eyes behind which lurked a travel-weary brain.

"How will I know the tree," he asked, "the whole place is full of them."

"It has a 28 sign on it, and a refuse container at the base."

He sighed, jerked the car into gear and careered off, while I nipped through the centre footpaths, down slopes and steps, and waited by his mobile.

He drove northwards two terraces above, returned southwards one below and I popped up the steps and stopped him on the terrace above at his next attempt. Four disorientated faces peered out at me.

"Nice try Panterpeople," I said. "let's go back and try it once more from the top."

All clients need are orchestrating.

CHAPTER 4

Our Wednesday client needed castrating.

Four children and a pregnant wife. Had I had a rusty knife I would have done it for him. Willingly.

A Courier's Reports are Never...

Bickerstaff arrived during the evening when we were not yet fully recovered from our tuesday's initial immersion into the joys of Children's Club.

We had ministered to eighteen of the blighters, wheedling and coaxing as we walked them the two miles along the cliff path to Kersludge beach after finding our local beach contained insufficient stones and shells for their infantile appetites.

"What's that rotten pong." shouted Hannah Philpot, her words belying her demure appearance as she created about the effluent left by the retreating tide.

"Yuck, aagh, yecht, grou." chorused the others, clutching stomachs and staggering about in mock retching.

"It's muck out of people's bottoms," yelled William Williams, who was at that age when the crossed hairs of humour centre on peoples' lower regions.

"Gruh, yere, phew, eucht," hollered the kids, tottering around, watching and encouraging each other whilst fastidious early holidaymakers

picked their way round them and cast us withering glances.

"Someone's bum's come off; it's all brown and runny," squawked William, reeling into the legs of a lady in a yellow dress. She brushed her dress as though contaminated and glowered at us.

And so it went on as we tried to distance them from people and get shells collected and sand castles built, but even that brought them to predictable chaos.

"He's kicking the shit out of my sandcastle." cried William, to the horror of a passing matron.

Eventually, the two hours purgatory nearly over, we scurried back past Hannah's pong and by the time we reached camp all was nearly forgotten except for the odd retch and peal of laughter which caused parents to eye us suspiciously with an 'offspring was never like this before you perverted him' look.

We had no stickers of Smartcamp Bear kicking the shit out of anything or wiping his bottom, so I gave them the one of him sitting with a strained look on his face. Then we rested and tried to surmount, the trauma of our reintroduction to junior bedlam.

- O -

Names are just letters on a programme until the people arrive; then the words leap into focus and a face can be put to them.

Bickerstaff sprang into immediate clarity with the advent of his personality, as opposed to William Williams's dad who was so self -effacing that between meetings I could never remember who he was.

A Courier's Reports are Never...

Sandy showed the Williams family into a tent without my meeting them, so there was a slight excuse for the first time.

During Tuesday morning's reception this weedy nervous chap had turned up.

"Excuse me," he said, "do you have a treasure chest?"

All our clients know we do. They read every line of the brochure, of the contract and of their tickets in the avid believing manner with which they devour their horoscopes. They know all their rights and privileges; what they are entitled to, what we have, and what to expect of us, in order that they can throw their weight about without fear of contradiction, i.e. without due let or hindrance, as they read in their passports. Being so uninformed, Weedy could not be one of ours. I gave him a brochure.

"Digest this," I said, "and you will note that we have a treasure chest. Travel with us next time and you can use it."

"Er, I am with you," he replied, "Mr. Williams."

"Ah," I said, nonplussed but recovering quickly, "then for a refundable deposit of ten pounds or one hundred francs you can join and borrow any of our toys and games."

"I don't have ten pounds on me."

"Fetch it," I said magnanimously, "and you can join."

He came back ten minutes later waiving a ten pound note. "I'd like to join your treasure chest."

"Are you with Smartcamp?" I asked, not recalling his face.

"Oh, yes. My names Williams"

"I had a chap of that name in earlier," I replied, "any relation?"

"I don't know."

"Anyway," I continued, "I'll enter you in the book and give you a receipt. What name was it?"

"Williams."

"Interesting. You're about the third Williams we've had in this morning. Must be a very common name. Are you Welsh?"

"No."

"Nor was the first chap."

I threw open the inner tent flap to expose our goodies.

"Now, what would you like? Ludo, snakes and ladders?" I looked him over doubtfully and refrained from mentioning the badminton racquet as I didn't want to strain him.

"Windsurfer," he said.

Our first Treasure Chest customer and the twerp wanted the windsurfer. I had suffered drastically at the hands of windsurfing idiots the previous season. They had bounced them off cars and into fishing boats, had been recovered inches from watery graves and been brought back by firemen. I tried to dissuade him.

"It's not rigged." I replied.

He blinked a bit and shuffled about.

"I can do that."

It was more than I could do.

"It's very difficult. Why not take this nice game of draughts?" I said, feeling that shifting the counters about would be beneficial exercise.

He squared up to me much as a mouse might do before biting into a lump off cheese.

"I want the windsurfer."

"Very well," I said, giving in, "it's behind reception."

I wrote "windsurfer" in the book then looked up, pen poised."What name?" I asked.

- O -

On Wednesday we ticked off the names as the people arrived. A trifle fraught from children's club and from worrying about that skinny client who had trollied down to the estuary pushing the windsurfer on our little two wheeled trolley, we were looking forward to an early night.

All today's arrivals could be here and dry by 5 p.m., we could get to bed at a reasonable hour, rise early and, with no arrivals due, shop for the aperitif party.

That's what we reckoned; but we reckoned without Bickerstaff.

"The two mobiles and one tent are in," said Sandy, "but the people for the other tent haven't arrived."

She had just finished the six until eight reception while I took my turn at preparing dinner.

"Don't worry," I said, dropping chips into the hot fat, "we will do our conjuring trick, it always brings them.

This was a simple infallible invocation. We would place hot food on our plates, raise a morsel to our lips, murmur the magic words, 'bon appétit`, and clients would arrive with the certainty of a genie popping out of a rubbed lamp.

A Courier's Reports are Never...

We watched the door as we chewed but nothing happened.

"What's gone wrong?" asked Sandy.

"Too much salt," I said.

"No, I mean with this Bickerstaff."

"He ll be here any second now," I replied, "you mark my words."

A courier must have confidence in his clients.

- O -

"Five hours late," said Sandy, "where is he?"

"Probably still trying to find his way off the ferry," 1 said, bitterly, "we should run map reading courses during the winter."

Nightfall had darkened the sky and our mood. I was prepared to dislike Bickerstaff on sight. Provided I could see him. I hoped it would be soon.

"Ah," said Sandy, as a large land rover loomed at us and slid to a stop. A fat head glowered out of the window.

"Mr. Bickerstaff?" I asked politely.

"Hey," he shouted, "is the restaurant still open?"

"It can't still be open." I replied, irritated by his manner.

"Why not?"

"Because it never opened in the first place."

That set him back a bit, he pondered.

"Well where can we get some grub?"

I looked into the loaded vehicle. His large, handsome wife smiled apologetically at me. His first day away, with four kids, surely he had food. "Didn't you bring any?" I asked.

"What for," he yelled, "we want French grub."

I thought that the site owners would probably dish up some Dijon flavoured arsenic on toast for this one but before I could mention it he continued.

"What about that auberge up the road? They still open?"

"Usually close the kitchen at 9.30."

"Lazy bloody frogs," he bawled, "but I'll try it." And so saying he withdrew his head, grated his gears and hurtled away.

A Courier's Reports are Never...

I knew on first sight that I would love him.

- O -

"What did Madam S say?" asked Sandy.

"Well, after I told her that Halfdone had damaged our mobiles she went quite rigid and uppity. Said they must have been damaged when they arrived.

"But she signed those sheets accepting them in good condition."

"I told her so but she said she had no time to argue with the driver."

"Have to accept her word. Did you tell her what you thought about Halfdone?"

"Oh yes," I said, recalling the painful scene. "I asked her why she employed the idiot."

"And?"

"She indicated that he is perfection, the sun shines out of him and, if he were not here, tomorrow would never come."

So we sat and agreed that Halfdone must be blackmailing her, that it was getting late, and Bickerstaff probably had an accident.

But the letter was a vain hope.

At half past eleven, he rolled up.

"They took a long, time to serve you." I said.

"Bloody wouldn't, would they?" he retorted, dragging his corpulent self out of the car.

"Then where have you been?"

"Went to that first hotel in Fouegenant."

"But their kitchen closes at nine."

"I know, but they agreed to make sandwiches."

"Did you enjoy your first taste of French food?"

"No," he shouted; "the bastards charged us fifteen quid for five sandwiches."

"The chef was probably on overtime." I replied. "Let me show you to your tent."

"Is the bar still open?"

I looked at all those kids crunched in the back with crumbs round their mouths. They were sorely in need of rest. The kids, that is, not the crumbs.

"No." I said, "it closed at eleven.

"Sod it." He thought for a moment. "Is the shop open?"

A Courier's Reports are Never...

"No," I said tiredly, noting his priorities, "why?"

"Because we need milk for the baby. It only drinks milk."

I wondered what he did for a living as well as breeding children. His sense of planning was haywire.

"I will lend you a litre of milk," I said resignedly, "please follow me".

And, keeping well away from his front bumper, I led him through the site to his tent.

But, all was not over.

I switched on the tent light and launched into my routine.

"The beds are in there." I said, "Double in that one, two singles and a folding bed in this inner, and that is a cot. This is a cooker." A thought struck me, "you do have matches to light it, don't you?"

"God, no," he snarled, "the wife never brought any?"

"I'll get you some." I said soothingly. "The toilets are in that building."

"It's dark," he interrupted, noting the obvious, "do you supply a torch?"

"Never," I said.

"Oh, god," he exclaimed, "the bloody wife should know that. She's been camping before. How do I get across to the toilet?"

"I'll lend you a guide dog," I said.

"Thanks," he replied absently, peering into the gloom, "which way's the estuary?"

"Down there," I pointed, "but promise you won't go there tonight.

"Oh, yes, O.K." he said, "but don't forget the matches."

I tiredly went back to reception wishing that I had a vicious guide dog that enjoyed the flavour of fat bullies. But, in spite of vicissitudes, your courier will go doggedly on.

- O -

I spent reception hour drawing a plan of the camp so that our non-navigational clients could find their way about.

As I pinned it up, a chap I had never seen before came and asked if he could keep the wind surfer for an extra day. I told him that some Welshman had borrowed it, but he could have it if it wasn't in use.

"And if it hasn't a leek." I chortled, which seemed to confuse him although he went off happily.

Dan drove in and after a quick round of dodgems with Hervé told me he was having to show the Mucus clients in as the relief courier had not yet arrived. But before I could ask him about his Hervé bashing streak he toddled off to chat to a client who was parked by the Mucus reception, blowing his hooter.

"That's got a nice tone," he said conversationally. "is it special or did it come with the car?"

"I'm trying to attract the Mucus courier," replied the melodious client.

"Seek no further for I am he," quoth Dan, "and furthermore I do find you attractive."

The man quailed somewhat.

"But first," Dan continued, "I'll show you to your mobile and, if you want, I'll get Pete to blow that hooter for you while we're gone?"

Madam S came trotting up with a fax from Head Office. She vacillated about, peering hither, thither and dither, then asked, "have you seen my son?"

I straitened up from drafting my weekly report and looked puzzled. "No" I said, "what does he look like?"

She gave me that exasperated glance which I was becoming used to. "My son," she said, "Jean-Claud?"

Mutely I shook my head, closed reception as she pranced away, and limped back to the camper. "What's wrong with your foot?" asked Sandy.

"I just put it in it," I replied. "Let's go shopping before I do it again."

Your courier is nothing if not sensitive.

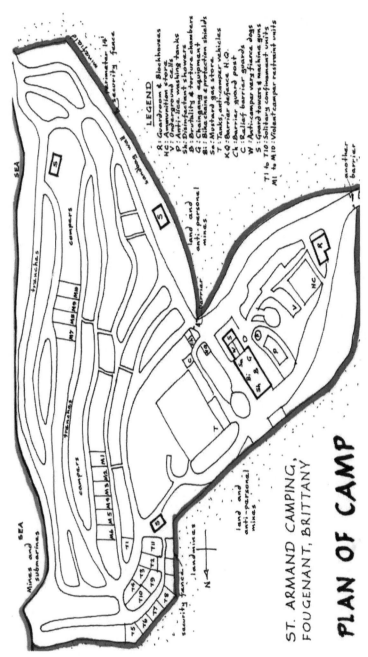

LEGEND

R : Guardroom & Blockhouses.
HC : Ammunition store.
V : Underground cells.
P : Anti-lice washing tanks
Sh : Disinfectant showers
B : Brutality & torture chambers
G : Chaingang equipment
Bi : Bike chains & protection shields
Sa : Mustard gas store.
T : Tanks, anti-camper vehicles
KQ : Barrier defence H.Q.
Ck : Barrier guard post.
W : Relief barrier guards
V : Anti-camper vans fierce dogs
S : Guard towers & machine guns
T1 to T10 : Solitary confinement units
M1 to M10 : Violent camper restraint units

ST. ARMAND CAMPING,
FOUGENANT, BRITTANY

PLAN OF CAMP

CHAPTER 5

Corentin, the ancient capital of Brittany, has amongst its notable features of twin-sired Cathedral, meandering medieval streets, half timbered buildings and remnants of city walls, three excellent and reasonably priced hypermarkets. It was to one of these bastions that I slunk to hide incognito amongst the shopping hordes and escape the feeling of embarrassment generated by the sight of Halfdone and his mummy. Or good old Jean-Claud as I was now determined to think of him.

And so we shopped for the aperitif party of that evening, purchasing many bottles of cheap yet palatable wine, litres of beer, packets of snacks, nuts, and sweets, pâtés, chicken, smoked salmon and all the ingredients to bind our reclusive clients into a cohesive whole.

Then cheerfully stepped back into unfiltered air only to find that rain had commenced raining itself while we were not looking. We had forgotten that our aperitif parties were taken by the elements as a direct challenge to their worst natures.

So muttering incantations such as "sod it" and "might have bloody known" we sloshed back to the camp site to ponder on things. Whereas sunshine and clement weather is casually accepted and used for relaxed dozing outdoors, rain makes you think.

However, holes appeared in the clouds, other than those caused by rain drops, bits of blue began to show and we decided to take a chance and go ahead as advertised.

We spent, the afternoon making sandwiches for the adults, hot-dogs for the kiddies, packing sweets into little plastic bags and generally preparing the entire nick—knacks needed for neighbourly noshing. Now and then a splattering of rain on our courier tent would advertise a passing shower but by 5.30 these had dwindled to naught and enabled us to set up tables, place bowls of goodies upon them and position ourselves ready to administer succour to the suckers.

They began to trickle in and indulge, each according to his

nature.

Jolly portly Robins laughed loudly and crammed sandwiches into his mouth two at a time. Philpot took furtive little nibbles at his, and a thin shy chap I didn't recognise, hovered above his sandwich taking nervous little pecks at it . Panter, an energetic bloke who came weight training with me in the gym at every 7am, chugged back and forth. fetching beer for his party and wearing a track in the turf.

At 6.45, having fed the kiddies on hotdogs, we sent them on a scavenger hunt so as to get them out of their parent's hair and their ketchup covered fingers out of the plates of snacks. This hunt consisted of three equal teams covetously marauding around snaffling various items as listed by Sandy, such as crabs, shells, spiders, road signs and other objects. Things they would have to roam far and wide for, thus ensuring that they left us in peace for as long as possible.

As English newspapers are expensive in France we always included one in the list then tried to mislay it into our camper. Another thing always included was a tin of baked beans as the French version is insipid and the English hard to come by. At the close of a hunt we would hold the tin aloft and go into raptures.   "Gosh, what is that, Sandy?" I would ask. "A tin of baked beans," she would reply. "I'd forgotten what they looked like," I would drool.

"How could you?" she would exclaim, 'it's your favourite food etc. etc"

Until the owner, shamed by this display of gourmet lust, would ask if we would like it whereupon I would fall on his neck and promise undying gratitude.

Unfortunately today's tin belonged to Philpot, who ignored the drama and callously sneaked it into his wife's handbag. Some clients never enter into the spirit of the thing.

Panter entered fully into the spirit, and vice versa. After he and his cronies had finished the beer he took to wine, fetching it by the pint in beer glasses. Eventually, finding the trek too difficult, they moved to the side of the serving table and, to help me while S was away distributing sandwiches, he helped himself.

From the other side of our crowd of clients I watched him sink steadily backwards onto our serving tables and disappear in a shower of crashing bottles and glasses. And decided that a) I would suggest to the Powers that tables should have unbucklable legs and b) it was time to terminate the shindig before we lost anymore tables or clients.

"Eight thirty, folks," I chirruped, "time to finish."

"All the wine's gone," I added for good measure.

"No problem," shouted Mr. Catchet, an interfering do—all, "I've got buckets of the stuff."

And so saying he whipped a couple of five litre containers from his tent, and they all climbed in.

"Come, Sandy," I said, wishing to disassociate us from the bawdy revelry about to approach a crescendo. And folding any undamaged tables we snook away leaving them to splash in their own ferment. Your smart courier knows when to leave well alone, pull out, and stash the loot.

- O -

"You are not allowed parties," said Jean-Claud.

I boggled. Parties were an essential part of the scheme. Not only were we instructed by Head Office to hold them but their revenue ensured that we could eek out our pittance and thus provide jam for our bread. Without them we could subsist only meagrely. I gave him my lofty smile with the superior raised eyebrows.

"For what reason, old friend?"

He blinked at the sudden change of attitude and absence of my former condescending tone.

"Er, well, it takes income from the bar."

I patted him on the shoulder in a matey manner.

"We are forced to hold parties by Head Office. You must know that. It is mentioned in our contract with the site." I said, assuming he could read but doubting that it was an accomplishment he practiced.

"Sorry and all that, but we have to".

He seemed nonplussed, "Oh, er, well." he went.

"It helps the bar," I continued, kneading his shoulder. He softened like dough in my hands. "We get the people together; they want to carry on drinking, so they go to the bar?"

He pointed out the flaw in my argument, "they didn't last night."

"Ah," I said, remembering that they drank all my reserve booze because they carried on too long. "Why not make a site rule that all parties must finish by eight o' clock. Then they'll have to go to the bar?"

He regarded me gratefully. "Gosh, right, thank you"

"A pleasure to work with you, Mon ami." I murmured, withdrawing obsequiously from his company and nipping off past the gym where Bickerstaff was training obstreperously.

"I say." called Bickerstaff, obnoxiously.

- O -

It was late afternoon and I had had a trying day. I didn't need Bickerstaff on top of Jean-Claud, on top of cleaning up after our first departing clients, on top of the morning's children's club.

Not content with getting stickers for the scavenger hunt, fourteen brats had arrived for today's meeting even though we had advertised sickly pursuits like painting, shells and rocks, hoping that these namby-pamby pastimes would put off the more robust boys.

But they turned up and set to with a will.

The boys were, at first, remarkably content. But, within a short while, they were

A Courier's Reports are Never...

demanding something more physical.

"Let's play hunt the courier," shouted one lout.

"Tie him to a tree when we catch him," yelled another.

"And throw buckets of water over him." cried a third.

This kind of degrading behaviour didn't bear thinking about.

"Certainly not." I said.

"But we did it to our courier last year." said the Lout, surprised at my lack of co-operation.

He was probably talking about the children's courier who was invalided out with a nervous breakdown and pneumonia.

"We will play rounder's." I stated firmly.

So we went outside where Lout clouted the first ball through the windows of Mucus reception. Then we retired out of harm's way behind the tennis courts.

CHILDREN'S COURIERS WEEKLY REPORT

Site Name: St. Armand

Date: 29th May

Couriers: Sandy and Peter   Numbers: +20

Venue on Site: Children's Tent

Advertised Programme: Tuesday: Beach competition

Thursday: Scavenger Hunt   Friday: Painting then Rounder's

General Summary of Week:

Ten children arrived on Tuesday. We took them to the small bay

beach adjacent to the site where they collected shells, cuttlefish, stones, seaweed and crabs; then on to Kersludge beach for more and to make sandcastles. At the aperitif party on Thursday evening we sent the kids off on a scavenger hunt. Most of them jointed in and we gave out 30 packets of sweets as prizes. On Friday 14 children arrived and painted the stones and shells previously collected. Then we took them to an area of

vacant emplacements and played rounder's.

Any incidents or comments

Tom "McCarthy has hay fever and whilst at the club meeting on Tuesday both his eyes became swollen. Or it may have been due to Judith Penfold's left hook. The site has a small volleyball court between two roads which is not very convenient for club games. So we use a group of vacant emplacements but will have problems in July and August when they are all let. There is no football pitch or field for ball games and the site is steeply sloping. Fat children roll down it.

- O -

"Come here a minute." instructed Bickerstaff.

He was surrounded by a bevy of onlookers made up mainly of underweight lads who wanted to learn how to build themselves up and respond positively when they had sand kicked in their faces.

His bulky frame was encased in a voluminous vermillion track suit, and he was seated on the bench-press bench, sweating profusely from a demonstration with the weights. The lads looked on in an overawed, admiring manner.

"Your brochure," he said accusingly, "'states that Smartcamp is one large happy family and we all get to meet each other and mingle."

I could not imagine anyone wanting to mingle on meeting Bickerstaff but I refrained from comment.

"So how do I meet people?" he asked.

"You already seen to have met people," I said, indicating his disciples.

He dismissed them with an airy waive. "Oh, them," he said, "I mean worthwhile people."

His audience accepted the disparaging comment with grovelling hero-worship.

"Like other Smartcamp clients," he added, obviously never having met any of the twerps.

"I invited you," I said, "to participate in last evening's aperitif party at which every client except you was present. You declined."

"Didn't feel like it," he replied, "when's the next?"

"On Thursday of next week." I said, knowing he was here for only one week as I had looked that up immediately on encountering him.

"But I'll miss it. We leave next Wednesday."

"Oh, dear. I am so sorry?"

"If you don't hold another while I'm here, I shall report you to your boss," he threatened.

"As you wish," I said mildly, and diverted him by changing the subject, "what are you doing?"

"Weight lifting," he replied promptly, easily diverted, "you should try it, Dad. Be good for you."

"Would it" I asked doubtfully, "doesn't it give you hernias and things?"

"Fallacy," he said, vacating the bench, "come on, try it."

I looked at his weights propped up on the stands. About one hundred and fifty pounds.

"Let's make it worthwhile," I said, turning to his disciples, "put all the weights you can find on the bar." I knew the gym only had two hundred and sixty pounds total.

He tittered to himself as they loaded the bar.

"Oh look, there's another couple over there." I said, as I laid myself onto the bench.

"Off you go, Dad," sniggered Bickerstaff as they were slapped on. I took the bar, lowered it to my chest, pumped it quickly up and down four times and returned it to the stands.

"Not enough weight to give a good workout." I opinioned as I stood up. "Your turn now, son."

The disciples regarded him expectantly; he settled himself apprehensively. "Lift the bar off for him." I said.

Two stalwart helpers struggled and placed the bar in his outstretched hands.

"Now." I cried and he lowered the bar to his chest.

I walked out to the sounds of him screaming and the panting of his attendants as they tried to raise the weight from his ribcage. Childish, I thought, but satisfying. In my heyday I used to press double bodyweight.

Do not mess with your courier. He may not be what he seems.

- O -

SMARTCAMP HOLIDAYS

Courier Weekly Report

Site Name: St Armand

Report N°: 1

Couriers: Peter and Sandy

Week Ending: 29th May

(Summarise your week including details of Weather, Site and Client Problems, Facilities

A Courier's Reports are Never...

and Competitors)

Montage went well aided by a team from Benemaas who erected tents and laid groundsheets. The stores deliveries were excellent and their organisation vastly improved from last year ; except for the much vaunted Briggsbox of tools which failed to appear but which was not missed as it contains no screwdrivers and is therefore of no use for fixing electrics. Sandy and I equipped and cleaned tents and mobiles ready for first clients due on 23rd May.

Due to site water and electrics not being available in some areas Fred was unable to complete water to 4 mobiles and electrics to 3. Also steps were 2 tread instead of 3 tread to all mobiles and I ordered correct from stores and informed Head Office on Monday that we required the maintenance men. Jonah arrived on Saturday and all work was finished just as the first client arrived thus no problem except replanning one mobile client.

And so we opened on the 23rd just in time for the first rainfall for two weeks. We filled 7 tents the first day, 3 the second and 3 the third. Weather was mainly sunny until Thursday when we indulged in a rain making ceremony called an aperitif party. Fortunately it cleared up before 6pm when we slaved over 32 adults and 30 kids. Best party we have had so far this year with clients falling about in all directions after gorging nuts, crisps, pate and smoked salmon and drinking enough wine to launch the Smartcamp windsurfer on. The client who fell across the serving tables had fortunately paid the damage waiver. All clients attended except the previous evening's late arrival called Bickerstaff. He, being one step behind, refused to come and asked us next day how he could meet other clients. I suppose every season has its Bickerstaff. A late booking, he looks like the Michelin man, arrived at 10pm, dashed off to find a restaurant, came back at 11.30 and wanted the shop. I loaned him milk and matches and tucked him up in a tent. Always one step behind, he has four children and probably wears a contraceptive the day after intercourse. But I like him. In fact we have enjoyed all our clients; they are an excellent friendly bunch and of the first five who left, three want to return here this season. It must be the smoked salmon.

Or perhaps it is because this is a very good campsite and the owners are most helpful.

They are always pleasant to clients and even to couriers ; our relations with them are excellent and they have given me a gym key so that I can let our clients in to train early, (Bickerstaff trains late) They have opened the bar but the shop and restaurant are not yet ready. I asked if they could supply bread and milk from reception, so the owner fetches bread each morning. Very nice obliging people.

CHAPTER 6

Our campsite fronted on an estuary, leading from a bay. At low tide the estuary floor appeared, a sand base slowly emerging from the retreating water and we could stroll along the seabed to nearby Kersludge beach, bypassing Hannah's Phew with a shortcut across the newly washed sand. After tides turn we would need to hurry back through the rapidly deepening sea, feeling the pull of the strengthening current against our legs, until the estuary became deep enough for yachts to sail past our site.

But the bay was safe for paddling and swimming and the sea, at low tide, increased the width of the long thin beach at Kersludge by almost a kilometre.

Fougenant sat in the centre of the uneven ragged-edged bay, its developing harbour a mass of yacht's masts poking upright as from an enormous pincushion. In the far hazy distance to the left was the town of Concarneau with it's fishing fleet busily plying forth, and on the bay's distant right was the small town of Beg Meil.

Sandy beaches and fascinating towns within easy reach made our site an ideal spot for all forms of holiday and our punters loved it.

"We'll be here again as soon as possible," cried the departing Mrs. Green, then dropped her voice confidingly as she pointed to the pictures displayed above our names. "I can see what you did before you took this job, Sandy, but," she indicated the photo so unlike me, "what were you? I'm sure I've seen you before."

"Before I had my face dropped, you mean?"

"Yes, I'm sure I should know you."

As they drove away, curiosity unassuaged, Sandy regarded the photo purporting to be her. Its multi-hued face peered back from between purple, blue and green legs, livid red and mauve striped boobs dangled onto her orange hair.

"Get rid of it," she said, "that idiot thought I was an exotic dancer."

"Try it," I replied, "there's money in it."

Her snort as she strode off told me she was serious so I changed it for a pretty nymphet in flimsy blouse with a peeping ripple. Sandy shook her head in sad acceptance but it was a hit, with subsequent children's clubs and older kids would stare at the front of her uniform hoping for sight of an errant breast.

A secondary effect was that fathers tended to fetch their offspring from meetings.

And, so as not to be accused of premature ageing, I changed my photo for one of a middle-aged fat, bloke on the telephone, who I was sure I had seen before somewhere, and then wandered across to the bar where another fat bloke I didn't want to see again bounced in.

A Courier's Reports are Never...

"Evening people, evening barman," shouted Bickerstaff, obviously sorting us into categories.

Freshly sweating from his gym visit, he barrelled his way between the tables to the toilet door, took hold of the handle and paused.

"Oy, barman," he yelled, endearingly, "you reply when I greet you. This attitude won't get you a tip."

The barman's expression showed that he would like to tip Bickers back into his sewer but he limited himself to breaking the handle off a beer mug.

Customers rocked in the swell of Bickers' wake then slowly

steadied and settled back to viewing the satellite television as ripples died from the tops of their drinks. Normality resumed and people became re-engrossed, the only sound, apart from the television commentator, being the occasional glug of a bobbing Adams apple as it filtered a drink.

But stealthy entry into this silent gathering was not Bicker's forte. The door crashed open and he erupted in like an antiterrorist squad bounding to the rescue of hostages.

"Pint of beer, barman," he bellowed, "if you're got over your sulks". He leaned an elbow on the bar and surveyed the room, "What's up? This lot died?"

"Should be coming round Hairpin bend at any moment." said the commentator.

"Motor racing," said Bickers, brain leaping nimbly to a conclusion.

"Can't imagine, why Mansell pulled into the pits on the last lap," continued the commentator, being the only person not inhibited by Bickers' presence.

"Load of rubbish," opinioned Bickers, "there's supposed to be a football match on. He took a swig of his beer, "now that's something worth watching."

"...to the pits to interview him," went the tele. "ha, here he is now. What went wrong, Mr. Mansell? "

The customers inched forwards as their hero opened his mouth.

"I caught laryngitis then broke my elbow', said a tall thin black girl. "So you had to cancel the concert," responded an interviewer.

The viewers went, "huh?" The tele went click; "...the lesser warbling woodnit builds its nest in such terrain," it informed the gogglers.

"I know there's a football match on one channel," said Bickers, playing with the remote control.

A Courier's Reports are Never...

"...and lace was made there in Medieval times," a red-faced man told the viewers.

A large, broken-nosed Frenchman took the control from Bickers and the tele changed again.

'...sorry it happened when you were leading," said the commentator. Mansell shrugged and looked impassive.

"He can't do that," Bickers turned to me, "come on; we'll get it off him."

I leaned across and shook hands with the Frenchman, as I had done every day for the past three days since he took up residence in the staff mobile near the dustbins. "Ca va?" I asked.

"It goes well," he replied, as Mansell faded in favour of a driver splashing champagne onto a judge.

"Here," Bickers wheedled, "give me a hand to bash this frog."

"He's a friend of mine." I said.

"Bloody hell," Bickers burst out, "it's bloody alright when a courier won't help a client. What the bloody hell do we pay you for?"

And so saying he stormed from the bar.

He had a point there so I helped him by finishing his beer. A courier will rally round when he sees a need. Even if the need is his own.

- O -

Another fat man appeared on the scene the next day. He walked gingerly, with small steps as though his shoes were full of eggs, and leaned backwards as if he carried a load of lard on the front of his waist, as indeed he did.

Our courier tent and camper van were behind the Mucus reception mobile which was next to the second barrier to the site proper. We faced onto the service road to the workshops and our reception tent was on the opposite corner to Mucus.

The man parked with two wheels on our reception site and egg-walked across followed by on equally corpulent wife. Then stood scratching his bald head and regarding the hole in the window.

"Bladdy 'ell," he said, "who did that?"

"Irate clients," I replied, "angered at the lack of couriers; berserk they were, out of control." It was the only way to divert him from the rounder's ball with its Smartcamp logo which nestled inside on their settee.

"We'll git Dan to mend it," he decided, and they introduced themselves as Sid and Sue, the Mucus couriers from "Pacific Camping." across the bay at Beg Meil.

A Courier's Reports are Never...

"My sister's coming to run this site," said Sue, "so in the meantime we'll pop over and see clients in."

"What about running parties for them?" I asked.

"Let the sods drink their own booze", said Sid, showing his attitude as one might display a raw wound. "Mucus don't believe in mollycoddling the bastards."

I compared this to the Smartcamp creed of smarm.

"What you do if they arrive early." I asked interestedly.

"Make the swine wait," said Sid promptly, "the brochure says four and I don't let nobody in before then."

"He's even made people hang about from ten in the morning," put in Sue proudly, "even though their mobile was ready?"

Sid puffed out his chest. "They don't trifle with me", he said, like a podgy Napoleon, as a car drew up and a woman hopped out.

Short fair hair above a harassed face, she trotted across to Mucus reception and hammered on the door. "Who's that?" said Sid.

"I think it's the irate client who broke the window." I told him, hoping to see him in action. I was not disappointed.

"Wot you want?" he demanded.

"The Mucus courier, we've just got in."

"Well you can just get out again, it's not four o'clock."

"Pardon?"

"Just a minute, Sid," said Sue, "if we don't let them in now, we'll have to come back at four."

"Oh, ah." replied Sid, idleness fighting a winning battle with his churlish streak.

"Do come this way, Madam," intoned Sue with the ingratiating manner of a wardess leading a client to the gallows, "all is prepared for you."

And, as she took them off for a first shudder at a Mucus mobile, Sid sank onto one of our chairs.

"You can't bloody win with some of the swine." he said, grinding his teeth.

Life, for some couriers, is a running battle.

- O -

As we brought Sid round with brandy laced with tea, a skinny bloke appeared carting

A Courier's Reports are Never...

our windsurfer on the Smartcamp trolley.

"Here!" I exclaimed, wondering what he was doing with it.

"Williams." he replied, whipping out the booking acceptance he now always carried.

"You're leaving tomorrow." I said, examining it and finding he was indeed one of ours.

"That's why I'm bringing the windsurfer back."

I noticed young William Williams with him and began to put two and two together. "He's your son." I hazarded.

"Yes," he replied, "we've just sailed across the bay to Beg Meil."

"But you've only one windsurfer so now could you?"

"He sat on the board and I sailed it."

I looked closely at Stringy Williams. I had fondly imagined that he spent his days pitching on and off the windsurfer in the estuary; now, to find that the runt could actually sail it when I had difficulty standing on it, caused me to review my outlook on masculinity.

He noted my mouth hanging open and climbed in.

"I'm the windsurf champion of Cornwall," he said, 'and I sometimes sail over to the Scillies."

Wordlessly I shook his hand, joined Sid in a brandy and revised my philosophy.

Do not mess with your client; he may not be what he seems.

- O -

As Sid and Sue prepared to leave, their new client dashed up.

"Your blankets are dusty. We went new ones".

"Who'd you think you are?" said Sid hotly. "Them blankets is OK."

"My husband has asthma; those blankets would choke him?"

"Good riddance," Sid muttered as I dragged him aside.

"Give them other blankets." I said.

"But they're all the same; all bloody dusty."

"So what. Give them the newest looking ones."

"Ah." he said, catching on.

"Oh, thank you, thank you." she cried, tripping away with the replacements.

"Psychology," said Sid, "I never tried psychology before."He thought for a moment.

"You know; I'd much rather smack them in the mouth."

Every courier has an individual approach.

CHAPTER 7

"So they were happy then." said Winston, the Heavenly courier, disbelievingly as though this was something of which clients were incapable.

"Well not really," I said, "you see they wanted to go shopping but the key wouldn't lock their mobile."

It was the following evening and we were sitting in the Heavenly mobile which doubled as reception and living accommodation. Fraught from the day and the horror of the morning's children's club we had taken a bottle of wine and ourselves to beard the Heavenly couriers in their den. "After all," as Sandy pointed out, "we'll be on the site with them all summer. It's ridiculous not to meet."

Our fraughtness was not due to the children's club being anything exceptional. The Monday one had, if anything, been worse as we were closeted in the confines of the club tent, due to a cloudburst.

This had not diminished demands by the smaller members for trips to the toilet and by the time we dried out from taking one another would be sitting with its legs crossed, insisting that we brave the deluge again.

The atmosphere inside the tent had been just as murky due to William Williams's fixation for anything insanitary. Following his lead the objects the children used as subjects for their guessing game ranged from toilet seats and bidets through to sperm and colostomy bags. Their knowledge seemed far in advance of their years due probably to the advent of television and keyholes. Within a short time Sandy and I had been vying with each other for the relief of the toilet trek.

Today's meeting had taken place in fine weather and so we could escape the close proximity of the rotters after the initial session.

First they streaked their faces with Indian war paint, and then made cardboard tomahawks which we sent the boys off to hide so that the Squaws could seek. The girls found very few, possibly because we were suddenly besieged by irate campers waiving them after discovering hiding places up their car exhausts, or tied to clean washing, or glued to caravan windows. So I withdrew with the boys to the tennis court which had a wire enclosure and thereby managed to confine them until their parents fetched them out on parole.

A Courier's Reports are Never...

Site Name: St. Armand

       Date: 5th June

Couriers: Sandy and Peter   Numbers: +10

Venue on Site: Children's Tent

Advertised Programme: Monday: Face painting, tomahawk run

Wednesday: Quiz then games. Friday: String Hunt.

General Summary of Week: Ten children on site and all attended club on Monday in spite of torrential rain. Unable to do the tomahawk run we had guessing games and then gave prizes for face painting. Sandy won which kept some sweets in the family but we gave sweets for the guessing game which made them keen. Also used sweets to bribe Bickerstaff's son down from the tent pole. Wednesday was fine so had the tomahawk run; boys hid them then we played tennis while the girls found them. On Friday we had a quiz and, after the weather cleared, played games; rounder's for boys and dice for girls. Many children will leave this weekend; pity as we always had a full turnout.

   Any incidents or comments: Most small girls cry when they leave at the end of their holiday. I think it is with relief.

- O -

"Did the bastards bring the key problem to you?" asked Winston.

"They'd seen us with Sid and Sue so we were natural targets." I explained.

"Typical Dickheads." he mused, scowling. He loathed clients with a hatred bordering on the paranoiac. He also hated children, adults, animals, tents, people with smart cars, and anyone who asked him questions or talked down to him. Persons in authority were high on his list and he and his girlfriend, Minnie, had not spoken to us because they felt that, at our age, we must be part of the Smartcamp hierarchy.

"So I forced their key in and the door locked, but it wouldn't unlock again." I said, then explained how they had gone off shopping in high dudgeon but fortunately Dan had arrived before their return and found that Sid had given them the wrong key.

Winston liked that. If a client could legitimately be inconvenienced he was all for it. I wondered why he was in this job particularly as my description of Sid's stance bred in him a desire to emulate and an attitude of worshipful envy.

"Cor," he said, "it must be nice to be older. Because I'm only 22 the bastards call me 'young man' and try to push me around."

"But they don't for long," put in Minnie admiringly, "he always finds a way to get back at them."

As we took a short cut through the hedge which separated Heavenly's mobile from our camper, we mused on them.

She seemed very young and sweet. When he smiled and dispelled his habitual scowl, his whole face lit up. A most attractive, likeable couple.

But during the whole season I never once saw him smile at a client.

- ○ -

Friday brought us little to smile about.

The previous two days had relaxed and coaxed us into dropping our guard.

Wednesday, the day on the calendar with a ring round it, was when Bickerstaff left.

His rowdy passages through the site always filled it and made us feel that he had been here forever instead of just for one week. His handsome, serene wife trailed about with the children but never with him. I wondered why she married him until I saw them together and realised that she ran him in with the rest as just another child. But after he left, particularly as we had few arrivals, the place seemed suddenly empty and I realised that I missed him.

We arranged no aperitif party because of the uncertain weather, and the small number of clients had attended the previous party and had met and mingled. Tickets would be difficult to sell, so we lit barbecues, clients brought and cooked their own food, and we sat around chewing, chatting and quaffing. And we ducked out by 8pm, leaving them to it.

We were therefore cheerfully vulnerable on Friday when the problems started.

"Come to the office." called Madam S, as she trotted past.

So, happy and relaxed, I went expecting to find a fax or computer sheets from Head Office. But she awaited me with a stern glint in her eye and a sombre Jean-Claud behind her left shoulder.

"It is not good enough." she said.

I cast my mind about for the cause of her discontent.

It could be the extra white lines our kids had pointed on the tennis court which threw players into confusion, or it could be the soiled underwear that William Williams left fluttering from the flagpole, or even the rash of tomahawks glued to the window behind Jean-Claud's left ear.

"You are quite correct." I agreed, which threw her for a minute but she gathered herself quickly.

A Courier's Reports are Never...

"The gymnasium is a disgrace."

I thought so too. The equipment was quite insufficient for a decent workout. It needed more weights, the press machine wanted adjusting and the leg machine didn't run smoothly. But before I could tell her so, she carried on.

"Things have been broken. The gym is not being looked after."

J-C nodded his head vigorously as though trying to shake tea through his nose.

I remembered seeing kids all over the equipment. I had removed them and put up notices stating that people under 16 must not touch anything. Also a cycle machine had collapsed under Bickerstaff's weight and I always had to rearrange things when I trained in the mornings.

But after 8a.m. I rarely looked in as the bar had another key and locked up of an evening. And now they were trying to make me responsible for any damage.

"I agree. You must look after it better. I meant to tell you that."

I removed the gym key from my ring.

"By the way, to digress for a moment, my client who trained early has left so we no longer have need of the key."

I slapped it into her hand and she yawed in a windless manner.

"Thank you for your kindness." I told her.

Thoughtfully she shuffled about a bit, which brought Jean-Claud to the fore. He felt it his turn.

"Your clients do not come into my bar. You have parties." He said accusingly.

"Last evening my clients organised an impromptu barbecue," I replied, having seen him skulking about, "otherwise none. On Monday you had two people in your bar, One on Tuesday and Wednesday and last evening four."

It was his turn to pace about. "What do I do wrong?" he asked.

"Nothing," I explained, "cheap offer clients put their infants to bed and stay in for the evening."

Then, to avert anything further, I attacked.

"My clients complain because there is no shop or restaurant."

He blinked a bit and took refuge behind mother.

"Things are a little delayed. The shop will open soon and we already employ a cook," she said, meaning the large broken-nosed man who lived next to the dustbins, "in whom I have the utmost faith."

A Courier's Reports are Never...

I drifted back to Smartcamp's reception happy in the knowledge that the day's problems were over; only to be confronted by yesterday's arrival.

"My toilet's blocked up and there's shit pouring into the bathroom." complained Mr. Pulley.

I sighed and sprang into action. This Friday really was a problem day. It should have been the thirteenth.

- O -

SMARTCAMP HOLIDAYS

Courier Weekly Report

Site Name: St. Armand
Report N°: 2

Couriers: Peter and Sandy

Week Ending: 5th June

(summarise your week including details of Weather, Site and Client Problems, Facilities and Competitors.)

On Friday, Sunday, Tuesday and Wednesday nights it rained heavily. The days were a mixture of sun, cloud and the odd shower but mild and the clients were happy: particularly as most of France had more rain, so I suppose that dogs in mangers are happy. Ten units left on Saturday and Sunday with a further two on Tuesday and Wednesday, leaving us very thin on the ground. With no new arrivals a party was not feasible, so we lit fires on Thursday and had a Bring and Barbecue which all clients attended. After the previous weeks aperitif party the site owners complained that we had taken their custom away from the bar and they felt we should not hold functions. I pointed out that on other nights their customers ranged from six to nil, so they backed down and we are allowed functions. Site owners stated that children go into the gym and had broken equipment; as they placed a table-tennis table in there it is impossible to keep kids out but their attitude was that as I had a key I was responsible. I gave them the key back and explained that Mr.Panter, our fitness enthusiast, has left. I train now outside in the early morning with my own weights. Bickerstaff used the gym with lots of attendant children and noise. He also made himself popular in the bar by monopolising the remote control and changing tele channels at vital moments. He endeared himself to the barman by telling him to be polite or he wouldn't get a tip. But when he left the site he amazed me by paying for the milk he borrowed and leaving a clean tent. Said he had a terrific time and will be back here this season; I don't dare to tell the barman. His daughter cried when they left and his youngest, in true Bickerstaff fashion left his jersey and become our first item of lost property. The owner is still very helpful, nice, agreeable and friendly as is her son, aged 25, who works on the site. Our Mr. Pulley moved in on Wednesday, flushed the toilet and had it back up on him. At 8pm the owner`s son dashed about and got the drains unblocked. I told Mr. Pulley he was back in business and we left on a cordial note. Shop should have been open on the 4th, and also the restaurant. Shop is being stocked and a woman is arranging it. Restaurant is having tables and chairs delivered. Owner says everything will open soon. At least they do have bikes and canoes for hire; and an empty bar each evening.

CHAPTER 8

She stood close, invading my personal, private space. Long lashes flashed across come-hither eyes as she fluttered up at me. Golden tresses waived past her shoulders and her hip brushed mine as she shifted to allow a better view of her cleavage. In the background Sandy sniggered, enjoying my discomfort. Edith was all of 60 years old.

"My sister said I'd like you." she lisped, her voice distorted by a nose job.

I took in the rouged cheeks, the dyed hair, the painted eyebrows and the false lashes. Strong corsets nipped the waist above flowing hips, a padded bra pushed up ageing breasts. I wondered how much of the original was showing; she was like a used car that had been reconditioned well past its scrap yard date.

"Oh, ah, yes." I gulped.

Mucus` renovated courier gave a tinkling laugh, feeling I was disconcerted by her charms. Her sickly, cloying perfume overcame the strong smell of the nearby refuse containers and clogged my nostrils. On balance, I thought, I preferred the refuse.

For a collector of smells, this campsite was an aroma-mine.

Quite apart from the defective drains that had campers holding their breath whilst using the toilets and had Mr. Pulley living with his windows open, smells came from the estuary at low tide, Hannah's Phew at high tide, Hervé`s mobile at any time, and the fish factory at Concarneau when the wind was from the south-east. It was no wonder that the training course emphasised the role of the courier as an intermediary between campsite owners and gagging clients.

"I'm going to enjoy myself here" said Edith, playfully elbowing me in the groin.

Not with me you won't, I thought, as my eyes watered and I moved subtly away. She followed me smoothly of though caught in my zip, and we tangoed about in front of her reception.

It is difficult to remove a limpet without resorting to physical violence but I was fast coming to the stage when a chop behind the ear was indicated followed by revival with a bucket of water and a concerned, 'good heavens, are you often subject to sudden fainting spells,` when salvation appeared in the unlikely form of a tall angular bloke with a scruffy beard.

"Oy," he cried, "Are you the new Mucus courier?"

It was not a description I would have applied to Edith.

Refurbished would have fitted better and revamp probably described her perfectly, but she seemed to lack self-awareness.

"Yes." she said.

"'Well when do you start children club?" He demanded.

She gave her tinkling laugh, which jolted him a bit, then explained the Mucus philosophy.

"Mr. Mucus does not believe in separating children from parents. He feels the holidays are a time when they should all get to know each other."

The man had obviously got to know his children and didn't like what he knew. His beard seemed to grow longer but it was only his mouth dropping open.

"No club," he croaked, and pointed a trembling finger at me, "but they have one?"

"That's because they like children," said Edith, knowing nothing about it, "but me, I can't stand the brats."

"You could still run a club." he said desperately.

She moved close, he stiffened and backed off.

"Why should I?" she inquired nasally, "what have kids done for me? All they give you are worry lines and stretch marks."

The thought of the intimate parts of Edith's anatomy turned him slightly green and he paused. She bumped against him like a shark feeling a swimmer before taking a bite.

"Mind you," she continued, "if you want to get away from them I could run a father's club."

She leered up at him with what she felt to be an enticing smile. "I know lots of games."

He raised his hands as though to ward her off and looked round desperately. "I think I hear my wife calling." he said.

As he galloped off, Edith turned to me. "You know," she mused, "a father's club wouldn't be a bad idea at that."

"Give it a go." I said, feeling that this would drive her clients into our clutches quicker than anything.

A Courier's Reports are Never...

Your Courier can be diabolically devious at times.

- ○ -

What should have been an easy period for us was thwarted by the weather.

Although Mucus and Heavenly were busy, we had no clients in our tents and only five of our ten mobiles were occupied. Due to rain keeping clients cooped in cars or mobiles they had time, as explained earlier, to sit and think; and the penetrating damp gave their thoughts the right atmosphere in which to fester.

Early season clients, travelling on the cheap offers, are usually grateful to be experiencing our expertise at minimum cost. But the weather keeping them indoors made them feel that they were not getting full value and they brooded on the various facilities, emphasised in our brochure in full colour, which were closed to them.

No use telling them that camp restaurants and takeaways supply poisonous food, that the shop is expensive and the Jacuzzi abounds with infectious bugs. They want to experience enteritis and pleurisy for themselves; they are of the unbelieving breed that has to stuff its fingers in the fire to discover what decree burns are available.

The only one who accepted the situation philosophically was Mr. Pulley who, each morning, left his mobile to smell on its own and fetched bread. The others trooped steadily in to us with their complaints.

Although the electrics were prone to short out causing exaggerated claims for ruined defrosted food, we were not subjected, as were the other firms, to demands for non-existent children's entertainment and aperitif parties or barbecues. We lit a fire each week and allowed our novice clients to ruin their own food.

And Head Office suddenly decreed that we must publish a weekly agenda of children's" activities so that parents knew in advance what treats were in store for the rotters.

This we worked to our advantage; for instance the television forecast showed rain, sleet, hail and gale on Tuesday and so our programme advertised a Beach Party for that day.

The effect was that the activities looked good but, in practice, only parents with infanticide or childicide tendencies sent their offspring.

But the other firms' clients didn't know that.

"My lot keep asking me to run a Kids Club," complained Winston, "say you do, so why can't we?"

"Do you have to?" I asked.

"Can if we want," he replied, "but we'll try to keep off it for another two weeks when

A Courier's Reports are Never...

our full time kids' courier arrives."

I would, I thought enviously, give my left cattle–prod for a full time idiot.

"And my bastards keep asking for a party," he continued, "Why can't they just go and talk to each other?"

"Try one," I said, "you'll make money.

"Ah," his eyes glinted, "that's a thought. I could give 'em cheap plonk and nuts and rake it in."

Sometimes, I felt, he didn't have the makings of a courier.

Just returning from a concerted attack on Madam S to convey our clients comments on the missing facilities, we passed a small, neat bearded bloke who gave me a chirpy hello and studiously avoided Winston. Each morning this bloke stopped at our reception for a cordial chat about mutual interests, even though he was not with Smart camp. A very pleasant bloke, I thought. I mentioned this to Winston.

"That's the Reverend Bristow," he said furiously, "a right shit-for-brains he is."

"Really?"

"Turns up, we shove him in a tent, comes bock, says the plot's too small and we have to move him. It's all extra work."

I had noticed that his supervisor had selected nice private plots for some of the tents but they were too small to enable a car to be parked in addition to outside furniture.

"So you moved him?"

"Had to. Phew, what an attitude he had. Very un-Christian for a vicar."

I could imagine Winston's attitude to the contretemps. "Did that make him happy?"

"Did it, hell. He turned up at our mobile, walked in without knocking, spread himself on our settee and said, look here young man, we've got a problem you and I."

"Did you sort it out?"

"Did we hell. I said what problem? He said, I'm not happy with my tent. I said, Jesus Christ, I've already moved you once. He said, watch your language, I'm a vicar. So I said, well in that case you'll know who I'm calling on won't you?"

Praise the lord and pass the ammunition, I thought, said, "What if he reports you to head office?"

"Our boss, old Rupert Foggerty, won't stand no shit from these arseholes," he replied, giving me cause to recall William Williams. "He'll soon tell him where to get off."

And I wandered off pondering on how attitude is usually a reflection from the top, from those above. If Winston was only the moon, I would hate to come under the full glare of the sun.

SmartCamp Notice:

REFERENDUM

After a referendum in Denmark which rejected the Maastricht treaty, other sections of the former European Community have now declared unilateral independence.

Therefore persons entering England via Plymouth must obtain a visa from the Duchy of Cornwall. At Portsmouth, permission is required from the League of New Foresters, and an entry permit from Kent Canton is needed for Dover.

Fortunately your couriers are able to complete all paperwork on your behalf and your details should be handed to them together with a blank cheque made out to cash.

Let Smartcamp smooth your way.

A Courier's Reports are Never...

"I think I have your ball." said Edith, sliding against me and running a hand up my thigh.

"No." I replied, "it's a piece of rubber in my pocket."

Her sun, I thought, must have been Methuselah's mistress.

I was fast becoming immune to her detractions, I realised, as she handed me the rounder's ball with its Smart camp motif. She was becoming part of the natural order of things like a headache or a grumbling appendix.

I had just completed a notice about a referendum on the Maastricht Treaty, as a good courier likes to keep his clients abreast of world news whilst they are on holiday and out of touch. One can imagine, for instance, the shock Prince Charles would have if he were a client, and arrived home after his two weeks cheap offer, only to find that his mum had handed in her crown to Mr. Major with a muttered, "give it a try if you think you can do better."

Everybody, even the Queen, must have their limit of tolerance.

Hervé had reached the limit of his tolerance with Dan and was parading around with a fierce Alsatian on a bit of rope.

Winston showed his limit with a 'no entry, trespassers will be persecuted,' sign on his door and I was waiting for the Rev. Bristow to retaliate with a notice on his tent stating, 'Forgive us our trespasses.'

Edith, of course, always went beyond the limit.

"Tell me; I asked her, "What's the problem between Hervé and Dan?"

"A lovely man, Dan," she replied, as bound up as ever with her own situation like a hen with an egg stuck, "but I wish he'd come with my pay."

"You've only just got here." I pointed out.

"Yes but I'd like to borrow some. Also there's a broken window in my mobile . . . ". But before she could enlarge further a podgy bloke intruded a scowl between us.

"You Smartcamp?" he snarled.

"At your service." I chirped, wondering who he was.

"Laidlow," he said.

"Were you." I replied.

"Am," he snapped, "Mr.Laidlow. I'm not happy?"

I could see that. Had we been holding an unhappy person contest I would have put my money on him without hesitation. But your courier is there to spread happiness not to win bets on client's peculiarities.

"How can I help?" I smarmed.

Edith melted discretely away like a blob of well-rubbed cold cream. Perhaps she only liked happy people and Mr. Laidlow was definitely not one such.

"I've got a complaint." he said.

"I hope it's not infectious."

"What?"

"Would you like me to translate it for the doctor?"

He gnashed his teeth about, which couldn't have been good for the enamel. Or perhaps he wanted a dentist, but, before I could ask, he changed the subject.

"I didn't want to come here."

Looking at, him I would have preferred that he were somewhere else, but your courier is courteous.

"Quite." I murmured.

"I wanted to go to Quiberon," he stated, naming a site about 100 kilometres down the road, "but I was re-routed here with only a couple of days notice."

We had received one or two clients previously destined for Quiberon as the site owner had been let down by the builder and the place had a devastated appearance that would be more suited to Yugoslavia.

I explained this to him but he seemed unconvinced. "And this place has no facilities." he said.

So I pointed out the pool, the canoes, the bicycles, and the bar. Told him that the shop would open the next day as well as the restaurant.

"There's the cook now," I said, indicating the broken nosed Frenchman carrying a holdall and walking between Madam S and Jean-Claud, "ask him yourself."

But he declined and walked off muttering, although he did promise to attend the wednesday's Bring and Barbecue, while I watched the heavens and hoped for the forecast hurricane that was due to dilute children's club, and wondered whether to get the Reverend Bristow to put in a good word.

Fortunately I didn't have to.

- O -

A Courier's Reports are Never...

CHILDRENS COURIERS WEEKLY REPORT

Site Name: St. Armand   Date: 12 June

Couriers: Sandy and Peter   Numbers:force 7 increasing slowly.

Venue on Site: Children's Club Tent

Advertised Programme: Tuesday; Beach Party. Wednesday; Scavenger Hunt. Thursday; Boules Competition. Friday; Face painting and Tomahawk Run.

General Summary of Week:

As you instruct we put up a notice giving the whole weeks events. On Tuesday it was strong wind and rain so most children failed to turn up on the assumption that it was not fine enough for a beach party. I would rather advertise a club meeting and decide what to do, commensurate with age, when they arrive. However we will press on with your system. So on Tuesday we had a quiz in the children's tent, and then painted. Only 3 kids there. Wednesday evening, at the barbecue, we sent them on a scavenger hunt. Thursday, every kid on the site turned up for a boules competition and afterwards we practiced netball then volleyball. Friday, we painted their faces (they did ours as well) and went on a tomahawk run. Then drew Indians with which to decorate the tent.

Any incidents or comments: A very responsive bunch of kids on site at the moment and all turn up.

Where did we go wrong?

- O -

In spite of the weather forecast of dreadful weather on Tuesday, we had dreadful weather on Tuesday.

Therefore only three kids turned up for the beach party with their anxious dads saying, "you won't take them on a beach party, will you ?" and then clearing off back to bed for a bit of peace. Or perhaps a piece of a bit.

With not enough kids to make it worth playing dice for their pocket money, Sandy played guessing games and painted rocks and shells with them whilst I checked that the shop was open, then passed the time of day with J.C. who was moving on to other things, having just half-cleaned the gym.

"Restaurant opens this evening." I said conversationally.

"We have no cook." he replied.

"But, but, but." I gurgled.

"We fired him for getting in a fight in Concarneau." he said, and left me full of disappointment at a lost opportunity as the cook could so easily have done it to

A Courier's Reports are Never...

Bickerstaff.

The week slowly improved, bringing out the sunny side of the punters but the barbecue brought forth no tins of beans.

Thursday brought another cook, a weak-looking individual named Louis, and Friday was marred by another children's club.

Another tomahawk run but this time, after we painted their faces, they insisted on painting ours.

Sandy looked cute made up with multihued lines and stripes, rather like the photo she had me destroy, but the kids stained my forehead white, put black and blue round my eyes and red above and below my mouth and on my chin, then led us out to look for tomahawks.

"My God." shouted Bristow, automatically calling on his employer in a moment of crisis as I stepped into the road. Mouth open he goggled at me, fought with the steering, wheel, swerved and demolished the Heavenly notice board. As I crossed to him I saw my reflection in his car window; I resembled a badly patched up accident.

"What happened to you?" he asked.

"It's Friday, dear," I said. "I always wear make-up on Friday."

Well; they think couriers are a bit queer anyway.

SMARTCAMP HOLIDAYS

Courier Weekly Report

Site Name: St. Armand
        Report N°: 3

Couriers: Peter and Sandy

Week Ending: 12th June

(Summarise your week including details of Weather, Site and Client Problems, Facilities and Competitors)

Our competitors are not competition. Mucus has no children's club and has not yet had any parties. Heavenly have so far held no parties, activities or children's club. Their clients complain and watch us with envy. Many of them will be with us next year.

I complained to the owner on Monday because the shop was not open. She said she had laid the shop lady off as there were so few people on site. Together with the Heavenly courier I pressurised her and the shop reopened the next day. Prices there are competitive. I buy my eggs and milk there which tells you something.

A Courier's Reports are Never...

The restaurant is being equipped but the embryo cook was fired before he laid hands on a pan for getting in a fight in Concarneau,(pugilistic cooks spoil the image) A new cook was engaged today, I think his name is Louis Borgia but I hope not, and the restaurant may be opened this weekend. Mr. Laidlow complained about lack of facilities. Transferred here after booking for Quiberon he felt deprived and grizzly because he only had two day's notice. I explained that Euposlob clients are getting there to find uncompleted accommodation but Smartcamp, being on the ball, rescued him before it happened. I think he was assuaged as he came to the barbecue on Wednesday. In fact every client came and a g.t. was had by all.

This is the owners first full year but they are beginning to get into the swing. They are still very helpful, nothing is too much trouble, and they drop everything if we have a problem.

There is a slight whiff sometimes when the tide is out. We had one morning of strange smell which I discovered was the fish factory at Concarneau and only happens when there is a rare south-east wind.

I told the clients it was healthy ozone and is included in the price. They went around breathing deeply and feeling good so now I wished that I had charged them for it.

Clients like this site. At the moment it is quiet and restful but in July/August anything can happen.

It rained on Monday, strong winds and rain on Tuesday, clouds thinned and were diluted with sun until Friday was a hot sunny day leading to happy but bright red clients.

We are introducing clients to the French way of life with predictable results. Mr. Robbins bottle opener broke; I think it was metal fatigue.

CHAPTER 9

Closely pursued, the lorry charged through the site, swinging wildly as Hervè struggled with the wheel and screamed incantations at the maker, much as Bristow had done.

"Come on, come on, Citroen." he cried.

It was a French make.

The week had started in a more docile manner due mainly to the sudden sunshine rendering the punters lethargic and reducing them to sweaty heaps, much as one renders lard.

A Courier's Reports are Never...

They were sprawled in random abandon wherever they were when overcome by the heat. Lying in the shade or sun by their tents, or leaking sweat by the pool, they were too dormant to bother us.

Foregoing the chance to cover himself in second degree burns like the others, Laidlow sneaked off for a quick look at Quiberon. Some clients do not trust their courier's word, having been fooled on previous occasions by brochures showing pictures of perfection with a glowing description of the mundane. A campsite in a field is described as having lovely open vistas, in damp dripping woods is mentioned as being amongst mature trees in dappled shade, and an old broken down camp is stated to have historic buildings of fascinating character. But however good a campsite is it cannot possibly appeal to all tastes, and the courier, as the firm's representative, is viewed as the lying culprit.

But Laidlow was disappointed at finding our description of Quiberon correct, stayed there for only sufficient time to have his car dented by a passing excavator and scurried back to apologise for doubting me and thank us, and the powers above, for rerouting him.

The Heavenly clients were not thanking their couriers in spite of the soporific weather.

"The bastards all complain." snarled Winston, moodily throwing stones at Hervè's dog. "Either the plot is too small, or the tent faces the wrong way, or there's too many tree's."

The Alsatian yelped at a particularly vicious throw. "Why don't they read the brochure? Preferably some other firms."

"Do they also complain about the mobiles?"

"God, yes." he snorted. "Bloke this morning asked why didn't we provide a shaver point?" The dog retreated under a barrage. "Said, it's all right for you young man, you hardly need to shave."

"Only words," I soothed him, "they can't hurt you."

"Can't they?" he said, "The bastards are getting violent; one of them pushed over our notice board." He glared around unsuccessfully for another target. "I think it was Bristow."

"Why?" I was intrigued by his perspicacity.

"Found a leaflet on the ground about removing temptation and overcoming evil."

And he moodily mooched off to overcome another client.

- O -

A Courier's Reports are Never...

On Monday Children's Club overcame us again.

In order to waste as much time as possible and to reduce their destructive energy, we walked the kids to Kersludge beach. "What's that dark smelly stuff?" asked one, as we passed Hannah's Bay.

"Excreted faeces." I explained.

"Oh, it's shit." she replied.

You can't fool kids so easily these days due to the insidious intrusion of scientific programmes on tele. There ought to be a minimum age limit for viewers.

Once on the beach we separated them into two teams and began to fire questions; but their energy was insufficiently sapped and their attention began to wander.

"What are they doing?" asked little Sinead, an Irish child with excellent parents, although in her it didn't show.

"I don't know." I said, and Sandy continued her interrogation with something about the Royal family.

"Who cares." said Fionnuala, Sinead's sister. Being Irish they might not have been royalists and I wondered if I had wasted my time informing clients with one of my notices of the Queen's weekend visit to France.

The DAILY NEWS

Monday 13th June 1992   20p

THE QUEEN WILL STAY WITH SMARTCAMP AT ST.ARMAND

A report that the queen will stay with SmartCamp at St.Armand during her tour of France was strongly denied in a bulletin from Buckingham Palace.

'Terrific' said Duke of E. bitterly,

'that's all we need to finish off the monarchy. They can slander Andy and sling mud at Charlie but this is going too far. We cannot be associated with a firm of such ill repute.'

HM the Queen on hearing the news.

'Sour grapes, an irate Fred Smart-Camp, owner of the firm, explained, 'Just because we turned down their booking as we don't want corgies in our mobiles. 'What they think they are; blasted dog-kennels?'

A Courier's Reports are Never...

But our quiz and the Queen took a back seat as the kids attention became riveted on two old dears dressed in black, skirts tucked into knickers, who were wading about in the low tide mud and throwing things into twin baskets. Goaded by questions and two boys who were energetically trying to fill each other's mouths with sand, we all took off our foot-wear and waded out towards the women.

"Yech, more shit." yelled Sinead, as we sloshed through the black slime of decomposing seaweed that marked the high tide line.

"And toilet paper." shouted Fionnuala, indicating wafer-thin sheets of weed on their evoluting way to becoming black slime. But by now I was beyond scientific explanations of natural phenomena and wordlessly led the kids at the unsuspecting women.

"What are you doing?" asked a child, The woman looked at her blankly, then resumed scraping in the sand with a little rake.

"They're gathering shells," said an English boy, "Aren't you?"

The French women ignored this foreign chat and stoically continued raking.

"Cockles," I said, as one sifted out some small fan-shaped double shells, "They're collecting cockles."

But the kid's television-bred knowledge did not cover the plebeian aspects that I had been brought up with. Cockles, in little round dishes and sprinkled with pepper, salt and vinegar and eaten standing up at a fish market stall, had been part of my childhood. These kids spent their free time sitting in armchairs and having their heads stuffed with theories, cartoons and commercials. Whereas we used to swing on branches across flowing springs, their practical sides were limited to the springs in their chairs and which branch store had the best goodies. Times change.

"Come," I said, mainly to divert Sinead who had her hands in the cockle baskets and was about to collect a French clout from one of the ladies, "let, us dig for some."

So we grovelled about in the mud and took a load home in Fionnuala's shoes. Fortunately for her age, she had large feet.

- O -

CHILDRENS COURIERS WEEKLY REPORT

Site Name: St. Armand   Date: 19th June

Couriers: Sandy and Peter   Numbers: 10 excluding us.

Venue on Site: Club tent, basketball court, nooks and crannies.

Advertised Programme: Monday; Quiz on Beach. Wednesday a.m. scrapbook & Games. Wed evening; String Hunt. Friday; Scrapbook, then Pancake Party.

A Courier's Reports are Never...

General Summary of Week; walked the kids to Kersludge Beach, split them into two teams of 5 each and had a quiz. Saw women with baskets and rakes sloshing in the mud of low tide so joined them; the kids collected cockles which we took back to camp and cooked. Wednesday: made scrapbooks of "My Smartcamp Holiday then practiced basketball and played "Hide and Seek. Wed. evening:

At barbecue, sent them on a string hunt. Friday: made the pancake mixture and got on with scrapbooks While it settled. The cooking was a big success with each kid insisting on tossing its own.

Any incidents or comments.   The couriers are fab.

- ○ -

With the practice we were getting kids clubs become more

successful and unfortunately all the Smart comp offspring turned up for everyone. The parents also treated us with a degree of awe because of the way we handled the kids, not knowing our success was based on intimidation, scorn, and downright lying.

Mrs. Hunter was amazed, when she collected little Charlotte, to find the child eating cockles which we had boiled on our return as a means of taking up more time.

"But she won't try anything new," she declared, "how did you manage it?"

"Told her cockles were the basic ingredient of chewing gum." I said.

She went off looking thoughtful and towing Charlotte who was demanding another trip to the beach for more chewing gum. But she still brought the kid back for the next meeting on Wednesday which showed, I thought, a lack of concern for the kid`s welfare.

This next meeting was pretty run of the mill.

We had the kids make scrapbooks of their Smartcamp Holiday, for propaganda purposes when they got home, after which they played basketball until they climbed the post and it fell on J.C.s car, then they ran off and hid while he hunted them in a vengeful way.

We kept them out of harm's way on Friday with finishing the scrapbooks. This consisted of more scrapping than booking but we later interested them by cooking pancakes, the only casualty being when Sinead grabbed the hot pan to toss the cake. Mother collected her without seeming to notice the bandage.

Because of the European Football Cup being shown on satelite, the site was reasonably quiet and the bar full, which kept the till full and J.C. quiet.

Until Friday when peace was once more shattered.

The DAILY NEWS

Monday 22nd June 1992   20p

RIO WORLD SUMMIT ON POLLUTION

A Smartcamp Admirer.

In his opening address at the Rio summit conference Mr. Bush, the American President made mention of the campsite of St. Armand at Fougenant. 'I cite an example,' he is reported as saying, 'of the worst instance of pollution in living memory,' He continued with a horrifying description of the interior of a Mucus mobile which had the delegates on their feet shouting in horror and demanding action.

A spokesman for Mucus said, 'we are aware of this problem which results from the type of clients we have to accept.' He stated that in a dramatic attempt to solve the problem they had employed Edith. 'With a hoover she has no equal and is a virtuoso on the mop and bucket,' he reported, 'but with our hooligans and louts littering as fast as she cleans, it is an uphill struggle.' Mr. Bush glossed over the foul condition of the Heavenly mobiles to cries of 'shame' and 'bribery' but did admit that a major factor in destroying the ozone layer was Minnie's hairspray. He gave praise however to SmartCamp for the superb state and hygienic spotlessness of their mobiles. 'These people are next to godliness,' he said.   **Help the world. Go Smartcamp.**

Elulia, the toilet cleaning lady, had just read my notice about the Rio summit on World Pollution, a subject on which she showed a professional interest, when hell erupted in the form of Hervé driving the site odd-job lorry in a wildly erratic manner.

It swerved from side to side, stuck screaming in low gear, whilst being chased by Dan in his van, rammed a flower bed and his van stalled, blocking the driver's door of the lorry.

Elulia stood watching unmoved, through eyes as expressionful as dirty black olives, as Hervé rolled across and through the passenger door and Dan burst from his van.

We watched as they floundered around in the shrubbery with Dan making roaring grabs and Hervé emitting terrified squeals as he evaded the outstretched arms.

As he escaped and hurtled up the road pursued by the panting Dan, I turned to her.

"Tough bloke, your husband." I said cynically.

"Yes," she replied absently, "I dread to think what he'll do if he catches Hervé."

Strange how thing's drop into place unexpectedly.

SMARTCAMP HOLIDAYS

Courier Weekly Report

Site Name: St. Armand
             Report N°:4

Couriers: Peter and Sandy

Week Ending: 19th June

(Summarise your week including details of Weather, Site and Client Problems, Facilities and Competitors)

Over the weekend this was the hottest place in France and the clients, done to a turn, were happy. Strong winds from Tuesday night until Thursday morning cooled them down a bit and gave them a chance to see the area.

Not many people; mainly ones who have been here for some time, so not, worth a Cheese and Wine as they already have friends so would not be interested to pay to meet people. Therefore gave a Bring and Barbecue on Wednesday at no cost to them and we provided the fire. Every family turned up and I am sure they enjoyed themselves even though they don't get drunk when they bring their own booze; which says something about human nature.

Mr. Laidlow, last week's moaner, went to Quiberon and returned sweating with relief. "Thank god we are here." he said, and explained that his original choice was not only a building site but plots were small and light aircraft landing on an adjacent drone gave constant background noise. "Thank goodness for this peace and quiet." he exclaimed breathing deeply of the ozone from the fish factory and pushing off to paddle in the mud of the estuary. He left a spotless mobile reeking of air-freshener, showing perhaps he wasn't quite so gullible, and a pile of books for the Treasure Chest, so he must have been happy.

At children's club on the beach we discovered that the mud is swarming with cockles at low tide. Brought some back and cooked them for the kids who went home in high excitement to tell their parents. Now, every low tide, the beach area is clogged with marauding bands of Smartcamp clients busy cockling and the evening air is rent with the sound of burping as they digest them.

The site has shown television every evening of the European Cup football and, without Bickerstaff here to change channels at crucial moments, it has been enjoyed by all. Even when England lost they did not prowl off and vandalise the nearby town which shows the quality of our clients.

The takeaway has opened with decent grub at a reasonable price; the shop is doing trade and the restaurant may open at the weekend if the cook can work out which way up the saucepans go. The owner's son had a haircut which gave him inspiration and he is now trimming the hedges. Last week they cut the grass, I scrimmed around the tents, and all is now not only spick but also span.

And with all the wading in the mud for cockles, our clients' feet and ankles have a wonderful complexion. Put that in the brochure.

CHAPTER 10

With so few clients our next week should have been a time of peace and rest. But your highly trained courier, being eager and energetic, chomps at the bit, frustrated at not being able to inflict his skills on apprehensive clients.

The Reverend Bristow was still around with his family and sidekick, or sidesman, or some such, which gave us, practice in grovelling and kowtowing ready for the following week's glut.

Edith tried to fasten her beady self onto him but his profession precluded all but brotherly love and her charms fell on fallow ground. Even so she kept ingrating and collected fresh milk for him daily as only long-life was stocked in the shop. I was with her when this came to light.

"Yoo hoo." she cooed as he hove, in a stately manner, into view. One always expected, from the way he hoved, to see him leading a procession.

But it was only Mr. Sidekick and a couple of entourages' who followed on his heels and they all hoved to by reception.

"I've got milk for you." she simpered.

I turned to her slowly. "I didn't know you gave milk, Edith." I said.

"Mooo." she replied into the sudden silence.

We even got friendly with a brace of Heavenly clients and baby sat for them as Winston ignored them after the initial confrontation which we heard through our mutual hedge.

"Why don't you have a children's club like Smartcamp." demanded the client.

Winston breathed loudly through his nose.

"It says in your brochure there's a club." client went on.

"From early July." snapped Winston,

"That's the full time one. It says – occasional club meetings— until then."

"Yes," said Winston nastily, "we hold them occasionally; once a month."

"When's the next?"

"When do you leave?"

"Twenty seventh."

"We have one on the twenty-ninth." Winston declared triumphantly.

It was such endearing comments that drove clients to seek solace with us, although we doubted that Heavenly's dwindling numbers were solely due to Winston's disposition. He must have had help from head office.

So, out of sympathy, we allowed the Heavenly kid to attend our next club; forgetting that wedges have thin ends.

The mainstayers of our club were Sinead, Fionnuala and their elder sister Maeve. Their parents had been concerned about the outcome of the Irish referendum on Maastricht, the result of which should have been shown on our tele one morning.

But the Irish are notoriously slow counters and the result did not come through on the seven a.m. news.

So as not to disappoint the O'Donovan's, I stuck a note on their kitchen window that read, "The Irish have voted - maybe".

The kids brought father's reply to a meeting. "Thanks," he wrote, with his Irish logic, "but is it maybe yes, or maybe no?"

A Courier's Reports are Never...

This meeting had advertised a Beach Party because the weather forecast was diabolical, but, as our clients had twigged the system, they all sent their kids plus a smattering of those of friends who were other firms' clients but who had worked out that we were suckers and would let them stay.

"No beach party," I said, looking at the rows of rain-clean faces, "I suppose you'd better go home?"

But leaches have nothing on kids when they guess they're not wanted and they clung on.

"Tell us a Story." said Fionnuala.

"What about?" I asked, knowing a good one about a commercial traveller and a farmer's daughter.

"Goldilocks" cried Sinead.

"There was this commercial traveller." I began.

"Goldilocks." said Maeve firmly, and the kids started to clap their hands and chant, "Goldilocks."

"Goldilocks," I capitulated, "came across this cottage owned by three bears and, being a compulsive tealeaf, slipped back the Yale with a plastic credit card."

"Hold it," said Fionnuala, "she just walked in."

"She forced the lock," I said, "broke and entered."

"She did not."

"Whose story is this," I demanded.

"Your's." they capitulated.

"OK; then shut up and listen."

With a cynical sigh she closed her mouth.

"Once in there," I continued, "she broke the chairs, wrecked the beds and, when the bears got home, they found her asleep in a bowl of porridge."

"What did they do?" Asked Maeve, interested in spite of herself.

"Called the cops who took her in for questioning. Apparently there was an A P B out for her concerning a beanstalk she had helped on accomplice called Jack demolish."

"Did she get away with it?" asked a Heavenly kid.

"No, they took her to court on a charge of vandalism and gave her into child care because her mother was never at home due to spending her time robbing sailors."

"That's not how I heard it," said Fionnuala, "she was a very sweet girl and the bears were nasty."

"That," I said, "was a story put round by her defence council in order to get her a light sentence. She was a previously convicted crook."

"But . . ." objected Fionuala.

"Listen kid," I said, "I am giving you the truth so that, as you go through life, you will think for yourself and get the right angle on things. Look at Goldilock's actions. She was criminal and the bears were the good guys. Am I right, or am I right?"

At last she saw sense. "Whatever you say, Peter," she said, "whatever you say."

But I still detected a note of scepticism.

- O -

CHILDRENS COURIERS WEEKLY REPORT

Site Name: St Armand   Date: 26th June

Couriers: Peter and Sandy

Numbers: Low; we had take in lodgers to make ends meet.

Venue on Site: Refuse Dump

Advertised Programme: Monday: Beach Party. Wednesday: Games. Wednesday evening; Scavenger Hunt. Friday; Painting and Craft.

General Summary of Week

On Monday, because of bad weather, the beach party was cancelled

and we told the children fairy stories.

On Wednesday morning only three girls turned up, one with Down's Syndrome, one dyslectic, and the other retarded. The one boy on site refused to be involved with them and went away so they made scrapbooks of "My Smart Holicamp Day.

The evening barbecue was cancelled and therefore so was the hunt. The parents of the three girls were leaving very early on Saturday morning and wanted to shop on Friday. At their request we held the meeting on Thursday when they painted and played boules.

Any incidents or comments

The girl with Down's Syndrome threw a boule at the plants in front of reception and broke a petunia. It has since recovered.

Heavenly are employing a full time children's courier soon as they are a considerate

A Courier's Reports are Never...

firm and do not want their couriers to have nervous breakdowns.

- O -

During the week the weather improved and the O'Donovan's drove off to sweat their way through the swelter to their ferry.

He gave us a bottle of Armanac, probably in gratitude for his children's improved awareness of life.

Bristow at last left, probably being driven away by our Mr. Shaw, who spent his days with his three little girls and his evenings preaching in the bar. There he sang hymns in counterpoint to the television which failed to have sufficient volume to drown him out.

The bar taking's dropped to a new low. And we met another breed of holiday company executive.

The DAILY NEWS

Monday 17th July 1992   20p

DO US PART

The furore over the imminent publication of a book giving intimate details of the life together of Smartcamp's champion couriers, entitled 'Peter and Sandy – do they or don't they?' was described today by a spokesman from Smartcamp Palace as a storm in an eggcup.

'Allegations like this could rock the mediocrity and affect the loyalty of our clients,' he stated.

A report that Sandy burst into tears after a lady client whispered in her ear was explained when Sandy said, 'the oaf stood on my foot and had been eating onions,'

Defending his decision to serialise the book in a pornographic pull-out of The Daily Nudes, the editor commented, 'The public have a right to know and we will show all. Public figures like what they are must expect to be exposed.'

It is understood that the paper will publish personal photographs of Sandy speculation that she approved of the controversy.

Peter however has remained silent although his friends deny any rift. 'He is his usual lovable self,' said one, 'his friendship with Minnie Heavenly is one of common interests. He borrows her hairspray and she uses his aftershave.'

In a show of unity the couple have taken a day off together but Smartcamp Palace has played this down as being normal.

'We don't want our couriers to be seen boozing and staggering around the site,' they said. 'It is not a good example for the Children's Club.

A Courier's Reports are Never...

I just completed a notice based on a headline in the newspaper which Bristow left me,about a book that someone had written concerning the state of Princess Di's marriage, when this loud bloke appeared.

"You're Smartcamp." he hollered, showing an awareness of which, at first glance, I would not have thought him capable.

He had a large lumpy body clothed in green shirt, vivid orange, red and purple sweater, corduroy trousers; had odd socks showing through soiled sandals, and his concession to the heat was that he had taken his collar off. But left his tie on.

He mopped his sweaty brow with a soiled kerchief, opened the large hole trimmed with thick red lips in his coarse features and bellowed, "I'm Marvin Mucus," banged his chest and continued, "see, I'm wearing our colours."

His sweater was indeed in the same material as the coverings on the Mucus settees which had clients wearing sunglasses indoors on dark evenings. I shielded my eyes and gawped at him.

Michael, our executive director, was a tall, suave, trim, elegant gentleman. Winston had shown me a photo of Rupert Fogerty, handing a cup to Heavenly's champion when he won last year's "most insolent courier" title, which depicted a frowning but immaculately dressed person of impeccable taste.

And now this back street market reject was claiming to be a colleague.

"Known ole Rupert for years," he boasted, "and your boss, Michael, is a personal mucker o' mine."

"You know Michael?" I queried.

He tapped me on the chest with a dirty fingernail.

"Course I do. What you fink "e does wiv `is old mobiles?"

I admitted to not knowing.

"Flogg's `em orf ter me," he said, "I respray, refurbish, `an improve 'em."

I said I had noticed that.

"I'd me own colour schemes." he said, not trying to foist the

blame on anyone else.

"Marvin, darling." squeaked Edith, appearing with her trolley full of the detritus of a departed client which somehow blended in with her.

"Little Edie." yorped Marvin, and displayed his lack of sensitivity by clutching her to his bosom, "my little baby doll."

A Courier's Reports are Never...

Edith simpered.

This nauseating display of mutual grot was terminated by a sudden kerfuffle.

During the touching reunion Hervé, complete with dog straining on rope, had been promenading along the path opposite. Now the dog, instinctively selecting the most appropriate spot at the intersection with the pathway from the pool, stopped suddenly, bringing Hervé to an abrupt halt, squatted and began to crap.

Hervé, with the embarrassed attitude of dog owners everywhere, stood holding one end of the lead with the grunting dog at the other and studiously avoided looking at it. And so, with his head back studying the cloudless sky, he failed to see his personal thunderbolt, in the form of Dan, appear stealthily from behind the toilet block.

Dan, having at last worked out that the appearance of his van acted on Hervé much as a starting pistol on a seasoned sprinter, had craftily left it by the site office. His cunning was rewarded by an unsuspecting Hervé with his back turned and with one bound Dan took advantage.

He swung Hervé round so as to relish the fear in his eyes, hoisted him by the shirt front onto his toes and muttered words of triumph about scattering pieces to the wind and kicking the shit out. But Hervé was not dismayed.

His face wore the shifty expression of a floored boxer who was about to rise at the count of nine and crown his opponent with the second's bucket; his mouth opened and he unleashed his secret weapon.

"Kill." he said.

"Grrr." went Dan.

Alsatians are noted for their strength, speed and intelligence and Hervés dog was no exception. With one look it summed up the situation, dragged the lead from Hervés hand and fled up the road.

"Ho." went Dan.

"Oh." went Hervé.

"Oy." went Marvin, having just spotted his other employee, "we're over here, Dan."

To Marvin physical disputes were part of his vocational training and it failed to register that Dan was shaking someone by the throat with the intention of inflicting G. B. H.

Dan and Hervé did not seem particularly friendly.

Dan however was unsure of his employers reaction if he were to distribute bits of Hervé about the campsite and so, with one final throttle, he reluctantly dropped Hervé onto the pathway, stepped over the limp form and crossed over to us.

"I wus jus' tellin' Edie baby how much I enjoy this nice peaceful site." said Marvin, as Hervé crawled painfully away smearing dog turd in his wake.

I suppose it was peaceful compared to Petticoat Lane.

- O -

A Courier's Reports are Never...

SMARTCAMP HOILDAYS

Courier Weekly Report

Site Name: St. Armand

  Report N°: 5

Couriers: Peter and Sandy

Week Ending: 26th June

(Summarise your week including details of Weather, Site and Client Problems, Facilities and Competitors)

Saturday brought cloud and rain, Sunday was cold and overcast. Late on Monday the sun came out to see what the weather was like, enjoyed it, and stayed. This campsite appeals to all.

Pity more clients are not here to enjoy it. Only 4 units let on average. 2 can't barbecue, one is a vegetarian, and the other has friends at Benemaas, so our barbecue was called off. We are even reduced to baby-sitting for Heavenly clients.

No problems except that bottle openers are breaking due to over enthusiasm or structural fault. This does not bother our Irish clients as they normally just break the bottle neck by hitting it on the window sill.

Our new clients are beginning to arrive. One has a fastback Toyota, inferior streak and G T shoes. I have asked the Camp Owner to put up 10km max speed limit sign to give me more clout when chatting to our fast-lane clients.

Liaison with the camp owners is A1. After previously saying that our parties were depleting the bar takings, they realised that no one used the bar anyway. So they asked one where they were going wrong and if their facilities are acceptable. I explained that young couples with infants tend to get the kids off to sleep and then stay home. They now understand this and we are working well together. They proposed a couscous nosh for next Wednesday until I said I intend to hold an aperitif then; so they will put theirs back till Saturday.

All is sweetness and light and our clients will benefit when they begin to roll in from next Monday. We will then fill up fast and are looking forward to it. Restaurant opens tomorrow.

CHAPTER 11

The peaceful nature of the site was being spoilt by people like our Mr. Henson who enjoyed demonstrating his fast car and homicidal tendencies.

A Courier's Reports are Never...

"Who's that twit with the fastback turbo Toyota g.t., f,i., twin-cam, b.f.t., t.d., with straight through exhaust?" asked Winston, who liked to be precise in his hatreds.

Another disturbance was the building work on the next door campsite where they were constructing a toilet block so as to upgrade the site to four star.

The sounds of machinery, banging, hammering, singing and blaspheming which accompany construction workers had disturbed our only previous tent occupant, Mr. Shaw our newborn prophet, who had nipped through the hedge to preach brotherly love and meditative silence.

With no appreciable result as his sermon was in English.

But complaints of the noise were rife following last week's occupation of three tents and Mr. Benson, a first rate prune, Mr. Peal, first time camper, and Mr. Moody, a full time grouch, spent many enjoyable moments bitching.

And with all the other tents due to fill on Tuesday with our special offer cheapskates, I expected more.

Fortunately the restaurant, takeaway and shop were now open which reduced the complaints, but a professional grizzler was amongst the Tuesday mob. Or rather preceded them, as Mr. and Mrs. Tallons arrived just after ten fifteen.

- O -

I had just posted a notice informing our clients about the Concarneau fishing fleet which, flying a skull and crossbones surmounting a French tricolour, was dashing about off Cornwall and cutting English trawlers' nets, when a large black funereal car that Winston would hate, drew up and this miserable looking bloke got out.

"Hoy, Smartcamp," he called, disdaining the use of Mr., "where's our tent?"

Less than three quarters of an hour later he was back. "We're not happy." he said.

I could see that. From the set lines in his face I doubted that he had ever been happy in his life, but your courier has to play the straight man.

"Why is that?" I asked cordially.

This elicited a tirade denigrating the cleanliness and construction of the toilets.

"Do show me?" I said.

So we adjourned to the bogs where morning campers had now finished abluting and Elulia was busy clearing their shambles and all was gleaming and spotless.

In a desperate attempt at verification he pointed out a missing tile, a dripping tap, and some leaves on the topside of the translucent sheets which roofed the showers.

"Come with me," I said, "this is serious. We will take your complaint to the owner then have the Michelin people remove this camp's star rating."

But he declined and, as he tried to scuttle off, I gripped his sleeve. Then spoke to Elulia.

She reached into her hair, clicked her switch and said, "what?"

"This gentleman has reported that your toilets are filthy." I repeated.

She looked in amazement at her gleaming ablutions.

Egon Ronay would have sent gourmets there to nosh off the paving.

"He can fuck off." she said.

It seemed that the flower people had turned over a new leaf.

SmartCamp Notice:

NEWS FLASH

The incidence of attacks on British ships by French Nationals has increased dramatically in the last few days. Fishing vessels have had nets cut and ferries have been boarded and passengers abducted.

Reports that some captured British travellers were forced to visit Euro-Disney has raised cries of horror in the European Parliament and the act has been condemned as 'diabolical' by the Human Rights Commission.

Some prisoners, whose release was obtained by Amnesty International, stated that they were forced to smoke French cigarettes and will now sue the Galoises firm.

In retaliation captured French pirates were made to watch tennis at Wimbledon, eat British un-sugared strawberries and drink tea, a practice stated by a French spokesman to be against the articles of the Geneva Convention, and reprisals are anticipated.

Therefore all British holiday makers who propose using a ferry within the next week are strongly recommended not to take valuables but to leave them with the Smartcamp couriers.

A receipt will not be necessary as your couriers are well known to Interpol.

A Courier's Reports are Never...

Having conned unwary arrivals into buying tickets for our Wednesday's aperitif party, after children's club that morning we hopped off to Corentin hypermarket to stock up with cheap goodies.

But our gloating was dampened by a torrential downpour as we emerged into the car park and sloshed across to our motor home.

And the drive back to camp was notable as being the first time we had needed the extra-fast switch on the wipers.

With the solid rain and the wash from lorries, our view through the windscreen was like looking out of the port hole of a submarine and had there been time I would have stopped to have a periscope fitted. But, before I could do so, the cloudburst passed and we drove into camp in only a steady drizzle.

And found a tearful Mrs. Peal at reception with her husband.

"We think we should transfer," she said.

"It's raining in the whole of France," I told them, deciding to believe the forecast as it suited me.

"Oh dear," she wailed, "what shall we do?"

"Get wet here" I said.

"But camping in this weather amongst these trees can cause fungoid disease in children."

"You haven't got any children."

"I'm pregnant." she sobbed, and her husband looked coy.

"How long" I asked.

"Five days."

I blinked.

He shuffled about a bit in an embarrassed manner.

"We had a cabin on the night crossing. It, er, it seemed, er, appropriate after the wedding."

I looked into their innocent trusting faces.

"You don't get pregnant every time." I explained.

"Don't we?" he said, "but we put it off, never did it before because my mother said, well, er, you know." he appealed to me, man to man.

A Courier's Reports are Never...

But a suspicion was beginning to form.

"Who told you about the fungoid disease?" I asked.

"That kind Mrs. Tallons when she explained how awful this site is."

And pausing only to give them copies of "Nuptial Knowledge" by Harvey Bedfellows and 'Camping for Clods`, I strode purposefully towards Tallons` lair.

- O -

But on the way I passed Mr.Moody.

He was carting bedding, suitcases and boxes, and stuffing them into his car while his wife slopped about wringing out clothes into a new muddy forecourt that had appeared by their tent.

"What are you doing?" I asked.

"Packing." he said shortly.

"Why?"

"The rain came into our tent."

"Show me."

Rain had run from the road through the soft un-compacted soil beneath their tent and popped up through the peg holes. I did a lot of fast talking, pointed out that the problem was cured by a new trench dug by Jean-Claud and they could not reclaim their holiday costs.

"But Mrs. Tallon said we could," he replied, "together with medical expenses if we get pneumonia."

So with a bit more chat and a final snort I strode on Tallonwards.

- O -

The Tallons were sheepish, conciliatory and declined a transfer even though I explained that the rest of France was bathed in tropical sunshine.

For your courier, the truth has to be pliant.

They explained that they like to help first time campers to avoid any pitfalls and problems they might encounter but agreed that this was the courier's job and they would desist from succouring the suckers.

And after trying to persuade them to attend the aperitif party with a convincing, "I don't suppose you want to buy tickets to our aperitif party, do you?" I left, deciding to make them the subject of a special report.

And met Mr. White.

"Excuse me." he called. His tent backed onto the Tallons.

"Yes" I said.

"It's about my bed."

"Don't listen to them," I said, "your bed is beautifully sprung with best quality materials. It is ergonomically designed and tested in spacecraft. It has been entered for a design award and was voted bed of the year by the International Invalid Association"

I paused for breath.

"Yes, I know all that," he said, "but it's too soft."

With some people you can't win.

- O -

SPECIAL REPORT

Site: St. Armand   Date: 16th July

Couriers: Peter and Sandy

Clients Name: TALLONS

(Detail the complaint/problem and action taken)

Mr. and Mrs.Tallons arrived on site at 10.18 on 29th June and were shown to their tent. At 10.53 returned to reception and stated that they did not like the site and wished to be elsewhere. Complained that the toilets were not clean or properly painted and they had found better quality when they stayed in a farmer's field. Also stated that they had informed our clients in nearby tents as to the inferiority of the site because the others had never been camping before and were therefore not, aware of how bad the site was. I was concerned that this rotten apple might turn the whole collection sour.

They said that they really wanted to be in Benemaas but the site was full and we were all they could get. I phoned Head Office and offered them six nights elsewhere and six nights somewhere else, but they said they wanted one continuous holiday, turned down the alternative and decided to suffer us.

I took them to the sanitary block and on confrontation they could not substantiate their claim. When Mr. Moody's tent flooded they almost convinced him that he should cut his losses and cancel his holiday, but I caught him in time. From being a rotten apple they turned into being a rotten pair.

They appear to be obsessed by cleanliness. They scrubbed the already clean garden furniture, bought a carpet for the tent entrance, and zipped up the tent to exclude neighbours children.

A Courier's Reports are Never...

I invited them to the aperitif party put they declined. At the party all the people from other tents stated that they would have nothing to do with them as they were miserable people and asked why we did not get them transferred. It seems that our other clients have ostracized them.

I treated them as though they were human beings and was sweetness itself to them; made no difference in my attitude between them and the others and even lent them an iron as I think she wanted to iron her groundsheet.

Conclusion: They may enjoy their holiday as I think they are happy being miserable. But it does show that a rotten pair is useful for binding other ingredients into a conglomerated whole.

P.S. I overdid the niceness and they asked if they could stay an extra two days but as they were still subverting new clients with tales of bad weather, I was sorry to note that I could not accommodate them. And so they returned to England to spread alarm and despondency throughout the land.

- O -

Bouncing around the site was Springheel Jaques.

A large, beetle-browed individual of some thirty healthy summers, he worked as a sports-master during school time and as a site animator in high season. Flushed With vigour, vitamins and castor oil he could be found galloping to the toilet, driving round the site in J.C.s wagon, or lolling by the small ancient mobile allotted to him by Madam S. He preferred to conserve his energy and use other people's, being used to supervising sweating callisthenicing schoolboys or overseeing overweight campers.

When he moved he did so with bounding steps and radiating energy, but preferred to slump out of sight with a beer.

Sometimes, in early morning, we could hear his wife working out on him.

"I'd like him to animate me." said Edith enviously one morning, listening avidly.

She was into hearkenism as she was not having much success with the active, carnal side of her personality due to an atrophied, albeit heavily camouflaged, sex appeal. Marvin Mucus had blown on the remaining spark of her sensuality for a couple of days but departed without closing the damper and had left her smouldering.

"Bit young for you." I opinioned.

"He's over twenty one," she replied, showing a remarkable range of preference. "I'd like to get to know him."

This was easier done than said due to Madam S trotting up to us with an invitation for all staff to assemble in the bar for drinks as a preamble to a site-donated meal in the restaurant.

"For you to meet the new animateur and get to know one another." she informed us.

Edith licked her lips as Madam cantered away.

"I wonder what's on the menu." I said.

"I know what's on mine." she replied.

A courier can be a bit greedy at times.

- O -

CHILDRENS COURIERS WEEKLY REPORT

Site Name: St. Armand
　　　　　Date: 3rd July

Couriers:　Sandy and Peter

Numbers:　building up from none on Monday to eight On Friday.

Venue on Site:　　　　Not necessary.

Advertised Programme:　　　　Monday; Quiz. Wednesday; Boules.

Friday; Model making.

General Summary of Week: No one arrived for the quiz so:

Q: We asked ourselves why? A: There were no children on site.

On Wednesday two brothers arrived so we played boules with them. On Friday one girl arrived. I rustled up the two brothers' and Sandy took them all to the Heavenly Children's Club where they only had one kid. They made a model of a dragon and though I asked a particularly ugly revolting parent to model for it, he refused.

Some parents have no sense of responsibility.

Any incidents or comments

Heavenly now have a full time children's courier named Cindy

Blackbird who is excellent but thwarted by their lack of children.

- O -

Edith's greed was not confined to sexual appetite. Her former comment about lack of pay was merely a shot across the bows as she warmed up her guns for ensuing barrages.

She developed a technique of pleading poverty, delayed paycheques, breadline living, and heartbreaking starvation that would have had a tax collector weeping and wrapping food in his demand notices.

A Courier's Reports are Never...

Her cries of "pay three weeks late", "where will my next meal come from", and "even my mice are starving" had her clients queuing to donate grub, invite her to dine, and leave fridges full of food on their departure. In the art of begging she made a blind, crippled, spastic Street-Arab look like a novice.

"How kind my clients are," she yodelled, as she forced the door of her fridge closed and sold the surplus to the shop.

She seemed to supply the shop with as much as the wholesalers and we were sure that clients often bought the same item for her three or four times as it was so often circulated.

We watched her antics with awe and jealous envy. "Our clients give us nothing; leave an empty mobile," said Sandy, "where do we go wrong?"

I had discovered that they gave surplus food to neighbouring friends when they left, or threw it away, or donated it to Edith if they came within her web.

"Clients see our camper and assume we don't need it," I said, "they think offering us leftovers will insult us."

"But we need our camper to live in." mused Sandy, recalling that Edith hid her new electronically fuel injected, turbo Ford Scorpio with power steering and reclining seats, as Winston had noted, between the cook's mobile and the dustbins, "how can we let them know we are in need?"

"Unfortunately," I said, "begging bowls are not issued with the courier equipment, and then wrote a notice for our information board informing clients of our dire circumstances.

And then we toddled off to partake of the free nosh and site induced jollifications.

SmartCamp Notice:

COURIERS

Peter and Sandy, Smartcamp's excellent, though modest couriers, are here to help with advice and information and are available, at the termination of your stay, to assist with the removal of any unwanted food and drink.

Peter, a destitute Lloyd`s name who responds to kindness and generosity, is also grateful for old English newspapers.

BACKGROUND

Peter: a European refugee, has just spent his last £300 billion on bribing Spanish officials, greasing coroners, perverting justice, plastic surgery, swimming lessons and bail for his children. As he has a façade to maintain plus 3 ex-wives, Sandy, various concubines, a bicycle, 3500 pensioners and a large overdraft, he is pathetically pleased by any handout no matter how meagre.

Sandy: a displaced Continental aristocrat, ex-Vogue model, former Bluebell girl and Playboy centrefold number sixty nine, has had her castle ruined, her lands devastated and her person violated. In order to keep Peter in the manner he deserves, she is grovellingly grateful for any leftover food and drink that departing clients may compassionately donate.

For your generosity, we humbly thank you.

A Courier's Reports are Never...

It started in a mild circumspect manner with drinks in the bar. I mentioned this to Edith.

"Really," she said, eyebrows raised, "so you think he's Jewish."

Her attention, once engaged, stayed in gear and was uni-directional.

We chatted to Louis the chef who was nervously downing drinks, Jacques who was nervously avoiding Edith, and J. C. who nervously had half his mind rehearsing a speech.

Madam S introduced Sandy and I to her husband, a stern looking man in evening dress, and we introduced him to Winston and Minnie.

"A right up-tight shit-for-brains this one." said Winston in a loud aside and Monsieur S's quizzical expression showed that he was fortunately lacking in English.

So I quickly inserted compliments about the campsite and questioned him about it's origins and he explained that he, a lawyer, had bought it last year for his son, Jean-Claud, because the dumbo was incapable of holding down a job or thinking of anything for himself and the site would save him from being a drain on the family finances and wasting his life screwing the local crumpet on the main berth of his daddy's yacht,

He didn't exactly put it that way.

With Gallic shrugs and hand signals he indicated that J. C. had retired early from half-finishing a university course, spent a year in London, another in Barcelona and, although remarkably competent, had playboyed around the vicinity until father had channelled his undoubted abilities into this venture.

And thus having passed the preliminary drinking time in informative conversation and cementing relationships, we passed on into the restaurant.

This was a large, modern, glass and tile room that echoed like a mortuary. Tables had been arranged in a U shape with space reserved at the top table for J. C. and his parents together with a few friends and relatives who they wished to impress.

The side tables were occupied mainly by staff, of which there were a surprising number, with the shop lady, a new waitress, barman and spare, receptionist and relief ditto, and various other nationals seated on the right hand, and us, i.e. self and Sandy, Winston and Minnie, Elulia and Hervé with Edith and a few others at the left.

I noted that Edith had shuffled the seating order, shoved Jacques' wife to the end, and dragged him into the seat next to hers at the top end, where she plied him with liquor.

And then the festivities, like Edith's mind, got into gear.

They were however in low gear due to the chef, who was not only cooking but waiting on, walking at a snail's pace, very deliberately placing one foot in front of the other, and swaying from side to side as he stared in concentrated fascination at whatever he was carrying.

His focus, though, was slightly out and he tended to let go of the plates of diced vegetables between one foot and six inches above the tables as he deposited one in front of each of us.

But we were in jolly mood as we laughed, talked and drank and merely gathered the vegetables from the tablecloth and dumped them back on our plates. Except for Madam S who glared at the chef and muttered "vaingret."

This turned out to be an oily, thin dressing and, as he swayed in with a large bowl of it, he met Edith's head suddenly thrown back in coquettish laughter with the consequence that she got the lot and he went back for more.

And when she returned in unseasoned clothes, Jacques and his wife were reunited and all our table had shuffled up one so, setting her sights on bigger game, she took her chair and inserted herself next to Monsieur S.

Madam S. never noticed as she was watching the chef who was clutching the serving door and gesticulating discretely towards the kitchen from which thin brown smoke drifted. As this was the province of J. C., mother gave him a kick at which he leapt to his feet and began his speech.

"Monsieur's et Madams," he said, "I have pleasure in welcoming you here to this dinner."

We watched the smoke thicken as it coiled above his head and he smiled round at us.

"And welcoming you to the campsite," he continued, as the chef tiptoed across his front, and into the bar.

J. C. looked around for inspiration and his eyes lighted on Jacques. "I would like to introduce our animateur."

The chef tiptoed back with a fire extinguisher in one hand and a glass of whiskey in the other. Madam S watched him like a snake weighing up a mouse.

"Who will, er, do the Animations."

Madam S. startled as a sudden flash indicated that the chef had emptied the wrong hand into the flames. Monsieur S also sat up suddenly as Edith's hand groped his thigh.

"I give you Jacques." went on J.C. and the animateur bounded to his feet and clutched his hands above his head as though he were a knockout.

"Anytime." slurred Edith, diverted from Monsieur S for a moment, while a hissing noise and clouds of steam drifted through, indicating that the kitchen was under control.

"Looking after the shop," said J.C., then named the surprised looking woman who hesitantly stood and took a bow.

The chef was plucking at Madam S's sleeve and she shook him off, much as her husband was doing to Edith.

The chef disappeared into the kitchen with an imploring backward glance.

"And running the bar." J. C. continued, giving due credit to the sad-faced barman who slowly rose.

The chef entered with bowls of ice cream balanced on a tray and we watched in mesmerised silence as he bounced one in front of each person, poured one down Elulia's shoulder and went back for more.

J. C. continued by introducing the receptionists and the waitress.

The chef continued by handing round ice cream until we were all served then picked up the pile of unused main-course plates and wove crab-like towards the kitchen.

He nearly made it.

Had it not been for Monsieur S pushing back his chair to escape Edith, he may have got there. Instead, he bounced against the chair, made the mistake of removing one hand to grasp the pile about its middle and disappeared with his load behind J.C.

We crunched our way through broken crockery to the bar.

"I'm sorry I forgot about the couriers," said J.C. having half - done the introductions, "but I hope you enjoyed the meal."

"We did," I replied, "it was smashing."

You can rely on your courier to tell the truth.

- O -

SMARTCAMP HOLIDAYS

Courier Weekly Report

Site Name: St. Armand
          Report N°:6

Couriers: Peter and Sandy

Week Ending: 3rd July

(Summarise your week including details of Weather, Site and Client Problems, Facilities and Competitors)

Clients are arriving by the bucketful and by next week our seams will be strained.

A Courier's Reports are Never...

Unlike Mucus and Heavenly whose clients are pouring in like rain in the desert. By next Wednesday Heavenly will be down to six units.

Weather is changeable and wednesday produced a complete day of rain. Rain, the clients point out, is not a facility illustrated in the brochure; so I charged them extra for it which stopped the complaints.

First really heavy rain we have had since we opened produced no problems except in Mr. Moody's tent which was on soft, filled soil. Water from the road ran into it, giving a spongy effect, and water ran upwards through the peg holes so I felt unable to charge him for the soft floor covering. Jean-Claud, the owner's son, made a ditch at the roadside which solved the problem.

Owners are kind and helpful, liaison is excellent. Workers are equally helpful and the perpetual problem with tent electrics switching themselves off has now been worked on and hopefully solved. Also when Mr. White told me he was suffering from our comfortable tent bed and a disease of the spine, the site worker gave me a thin plastic door from which I removed the hinges and used to make a hard mattress base. Mr. White is happy, sleeping well and a nice chap so I failed to charge him extra for the service.

Site owners gave all staff and couriers drinks in the bar and a snack in the restaurant one evening so that we could get to know one another and meet the animateur. A good friendly evening, but the cook, who was serving, got drunk and, to the tight-lipped annoyance of the owner's wife, began to drop things. He dropped vaingret down the Mucus lady, who went home and changed. Spilt ice cream over the toilet cleaning lady, leaving clean marks on her dress, and for an encore fell over whilst carrying a pile of plates. Next morning saw him being escorted from the camp, carrying a valise and holding his head, and the assistant cook is carrying on while the owners try to find a cook who does not fight or drink and has more than thumbs on his hands.

Even we use the takeaway which is excellent, popular and cheap and the restaurant has the same menu which the clients are very happy with. They were also happy with our aperitif party which we held in the gym due to inclement weather, and all but two families attended.

No incidents this week except that Mrs. Hollocaust fell over our potted plant. I dread to think of the state of her husband's market garden.

CHAPTER 12

It was midweek when Dan crept into camp wearing plimsolls on silent feet and a cunning expression on be-whiskered face.

A Courier's Reports are Never...

We were just knocking off for lunch after having suffered, for two hours, a combination of our kids and Heavenly`s. The mixture by no means diluted our boisterous swine and, if anything, rivalry added to the bedlam.

"It's the way you treat them," said Cindy Birdsong, primed by a university degree in child psychology and another in general autopsy. A true professional, she could take a kid to pieces mentally or physically.

"I only tell them how rotten they are," I protested, "I work on a need to know basis."

"You provoke them." she replied, giving me a sudden insight into why they crawled all over me.

I had therefore become somewhat stern and authoritative until two of Mr. Yukkies sons with a revolting, "sod this, we're pissing off," had folded their possessions in mid-club and galloped away to plague mum and dad. So I relented and the others began to jump up and down on me once more.

With kids there seems to be no middle course.

And our club meetings were becoming heavily overloaded due to a special offer filling all the mobiles. And the tents were not only full but we were asked by Head Office to find places for a further two.

Fortunately Madam S told me that in July and August the site was fully pre-booked and she could only let us have the one, next to the toilet block, that fronted a septic tank.

So Sandy and I, early in the week, had erected another tent which was now graced by the Yukkies.

Mr. Yukkie was a vacant man with staring eyes beneath permanently raised eyebrows; his wife a skinny thing with long thin blonde hair and eyes so close together that the left one was probably on the right. This unprepossessing pair had produced four children, probably driven together in close union because no one else would have anything to do with either of them.

Edith was in the same boat, except that she was single, having worn out three husbands and consigned them to various assorted crematoria; but she surmounted her loneliness by leaping out at unsuspecting men.

One such was our client Mr. McClay. A friendly gregarious man he was easy prey to Edith's tentacles. As he staggered off after being accosted and having her rub against him, she caught my eye, waived a sweeping hand to embrace the Mucus forecourt and cried, "I've got a mantrap hidden here."

"I thought you were the mantrap." I replied, in an attempt to put her off me for a while.

A Courier's Reports are Never...

But, to no avail.

She had nipped across and was groping me for a bit of practice when Madam S jogged up.

"The English do not come to our functions," she commented.

"You hold everything in French," I replied, having listened in to Bingo, Snap, and Musical Frogs all in Foreign, "they do not understand."

"Such ignorance," she commented, "if they came they would learn"

"You even post the notices in French." I said, having seen our clients scratching their heads over a poster on the craphouse wall.

"Then why do they come to France?"

"To search for cafés that make tea, chip butties and other such signs of civilised culture." I told her.

But you can't instil a nation's attitude into an unreceptive Frog in one sentence and she trotted off in a preoccupied puzzled way.

Her son, after ejecting a heavily hung-over chef with bandaged hands, had tried to sublet the restaurant to a friend with avaricious tendencies but, on finding a bunch of campers around the proposed expensive menu laughing with derision and boycott, had shelved the idea and made the assistant chef serve both the takeaway and the restaurant.

And now here was Dan, working on a wheeze that the word take-away had fomented.

- O -

CHILDRENS COURIER WEEKLY REPORT

Site Name: St. Armand   Date: 10th July

Couriers: Sandy and Peter   Numbers: Building fast

Venue on Site: Children's Tent

Advertised Programme: Monday: Beach Games. Wednesday: Collage . Friday: Sports Day.

General Summary of Week: Monday; combined with Heavenly to play rounders on beach as they have few kids and we therefore had a better chance of winning. Thus demonstrating to our lot that life is unfair and you should never give the other bloke an equal chance.

Wednesday; again combined; 15 kids plus 8 of Heavenlys. Made collage of underwater scene with seaweed, shells, dead crabs, fish bones and defunct snails. The tent smells funny.

A Courier's Reports are Never...

Friday; had sports day on the beach; played dodge the rain showers, relay race, wheelbarrow race and skimming stones at passing canoeists. 11 kids turned up and, being idle swine, hated every minute. What we really need is a professional kid's courier like Cindy Birdsong.

Any incidents or comments

Louise got sand in her shoes and I carried her home. You asked why Bickerstaff's son climbed the tent pole; it is because he is a chip off the old baboon.

The DAILY NEWS

Monday 12th July 1992   20p

AIDS SCARE

Two old aged pensioners in Newcastle yesterday had their left ears burnt when lightning struck their hearing aids during a storm.

'I was terrified; said a senile onlooker, 'They lit up like Christmas trees and smelt like roasting turkey. It quite took me aback to me childhood.

A spokesman for the manufactures denied that there was a fault in their design but recommended that all users be earthed through circuit breakers. 'We will provide little trolleys so that the equipment can be towed behind Zimmer frames; he told concerned health officials, 'But in the meantime people should not bathe or climb pylons whilst wearing them.'

'I am too scared to switch on my hearing aid,' stated Edith Knockers, a former miner. When asked if she had personally experienced problems she replied, 'What?'

A electric pilon 2 days ago.

A Courier's Reports are Never...

I regarded Dan with interest as I posted up a notice prompted by a newspaper headline about an Aids scare, and tried to fathom his intent.

"Takeaway" he sniggered, waiving two planks of wood into which he had pre-drilled holes. "Where's Hervé?"

Hervé always had, in his mobile, a short midday siesta brought on by fatigue, lethargy and drinking his lunch to fast.

I told Dan so and he nodded in confirmation. But I also knew that Hervé kept his door locked and had bars fitted across the windows so as not to be surprised by a vengeful Dan.

I chewed a meditative French salami as I watched to see how these precautions would be breeched.

But Dan made no attempt to breach any defences except the Alsatian at which he glowered.

The dog slunk off in a beaten manner and went in search of the animateur's toy poodle on which to vent its frustration, while Dan with his plank and a well-oiled screwdriver quietly screwed the mobile door firmly fixed. Then, having completed part one of the operation, rubbed his hands and sniggered off back to his van, parked by the entrance.

Most noise was being generated by Sandy and myself chewing salami as the adjacent site's building workers had knocked off for lunch, when Dan, entering phase two, coasted his van silently backwards down the slight incline towards the mobile.

Being used to dragging mobiles onto sites he knew exactly the length of his van and the position of the tow bar and stopped with it less than one millimetre from the mobile hitch.

And climbed out for phase 3.

It was the work of a moment for him to grasp the hitch, jerk it onto his tow bar, leap into the van, start the engine and roar off towards the entrance.

Sound, which had been holding its breath, now erupted at full volume.

The water and sewer pipe connections and the mobile's supporting timbers broke, giving off snapping cracks like the starter of a race who, tired of the single bang of his pistol, had decided to do it with a machine gun.

The mobile lurched from its blocks, dropped onto rusted wheels and, with deflated tyres flapping, hurried after Dan's van.

The entrance road, having been surfaced by J. C. on one of his many bits of equipment, was only half made up and it's corrugations together with the steadily increasing speed of the van, shook loose all the innards of the mobile, which had never

93

been packed for movement.

Breaking crockery competed with crashing furniture and the groaning of the ungreased chassis, and the cries of Hervé were lost in the din as he appeared at the rear window and not only watched the world go by, but saw his disintegrate.

And as we goggled, mouths open and salami un-chewed, Hervé disappeared to add door pounding to the din.

"I wonder where Dan's taking him," said Sandy, as the racket, passed through the site entrance.

The thought had crossed my mind.

Dan was a practical man with an inventive streak. Stir these qualities together with anger, vindictiveness and revenge and one had a very potent, explosive mixture. So, hoping to see the pyrotechnics, I nipped up onto the camper roof and watched over the hedge.

The road from the campsite curved along the cliff top and at one point gave onto a picnic spot much favoured by sightseers, who enjoyed the view over the bay, and courting couples who preferred the view inside their cars. It was here that Dan drew up, reversed, and ran round to unhitch the mobile.

But as he strained the freed mobile towards the cliff edge, Hervé popped up through the roof vent like a claustrophobic rabbit from a hat when the conjurors back is turned, leapt onto the ground, rolled about a bit, picked himself up and frenziedly ran to the sanctuary of the campsite.

And Dan, hearing his fleeing steps, stopped, turned and stood howling with frustration like a wolf who sees his lunch scarpering, then moodily, being a thrifty man, unscrewed his planks from the door.

But the episode was by no means over. The door was flung open and out erupted Elulia.

It has been noted by ancient chroniclers that the female is deadlier than the male. In Dan's case this took a bit of doing but Elulia managed it. With an anger born of seeing the inside of her home wrecked, she stepped smartly up to Dan and felled him with a lump of timber that originally had formed part of her dressing table.

And Dan, overcome by suddenly seeing his loved one and being smitten, lay bleeding upon the ground and excused his conduct.

"I didn't know you were in there." he said.

It had always been Elulia`s practice to shower after her

morning`s toil and partake of fresh air in a hammock strung between the refuse containers. This deviation from ritual she now explained.

"I was in the bloody crapper, wasn't I." she shouted.

And ignoring Dan's plea that it was only his way of demonstrating he cared, she belted him once more with the balk and stormed off to unfinished business.

Arriving back from lunch, Madam S approached me in a puzzled manner.

"Why is Hervé's mobile by the cliff edge?" she asked.

"He wants to experience a change of outlook." I replied.

And wondered what other fireworks were in store.

- O -

SMARTCAMP HOLIDAYS

Courier Weekly Report

Site Name: St. Armand   Report N°: 7

Couriers: Peter and Sandy

Week Ending: 10th July

(Summarise your week including details of Weather, Site and Client Problems, Facilities and Competitors)

Rain Friday night cleared to sun and showers on Saturday, building to a hot sunny day on Tuesday with sun and showers on

other days. This however did not register with the painful subversive Tallons who left telling newcomers that they had only 2 days of sun during their 12 days holiday and tried to cajole people into going home every time it rained. They almost convinced the Moodys who only stayed on in order to reduce their tent to a hovel, which took us both over two hours to clean and disinfect, and seem to have influenced the Yukkies who are so unreal that they deserve a special report all to themselves. The latter are staying in the new extra tent which we erected and equipped just prior to their arrival and, judging by their appearance, will look ancient and decrepit when they leave. But most of our clients are clean, healthy, and eminently suited to the task of representing Smartcamp. We have a nice bunch here at the moment.

Unfortunately we couldn't mix with them on wednesday as our aperitif party received little response being too near the previous, but we visit, socialise, and have them round for drinks.

All site facilities are now open as a new chef has been engaged, and clients seem happy with them. The owners are still helpful but hurtling hither and thither in frantic French fashion as the number of campers builds up.

A Courier's Reports are Never...

Heavenly have few clients at the moment and Mucus ditto. An animateur is working for the site but as everything is done in French most of our kids don't go and prefer to torment us at the Smartcamp Junior Jailbird Klub.

For entertainment, the Odd Job man's Alsatian savaged the toy noodle of the animateur. As the animrteur only speaks to Hervé when presenting vet's bills, the site is again reasonably peaceful.

- O -

SPECIAL REPORT

Site: St. Armand

Date: 14th July

Couriers: Peter and Sandy

Clients Name: Mr. Yukkies

(Detail the complaint/problem and action taken)

Mother, father and four crew-cut boys aged 10, 8, 8 and 6 were put into our brand new tent number 11. On their first day they went to Corentin hypermarket and were given 150 francs each to spend, which they used to purchase super soakers. They then spent the day on camp soaking each other until, with most of their holiday clothes wet, the parents removed the soakers and gave them a large dingy to play with. They took this to the estuary, fell out and drenched the rest of their clothes.

As it was showery, father requested a transfer to anywhere sunny in order to dry them out and said that the boys had been up all night with bad coughs. They repeated the soaker episode next day including the "up all night" bit. Father stated that one child had a weak membrane in his heart and a dose of pneumonia could kill him. I think father had a week membrane in the head as, immediately after our chat, Sandy saw the kids again soaking each other.

Being high season I could not get them a transfer. Father said he thought they should all go home as they had a tumble dryer there, mother said she would be happier at home with her washing machine. Father asked me if I thought that a French doctor would give him a certificate to say that the kid with the weak heart had to go home, so that he could claim the return fare from the insurance.

They finally booked onto a Roscof ferry and dashed off with the final comment, "by the way, it is very noisy in this tent and we were kept awake until 3 a.m. by children playing in the toilet block. They may use this after-thought to try to claim a refund from us.

Father had the endearing habit of prefacing every comment with the words, "this is no reflection on you, you understand, but . . ."

I tried to transfer them to sunny Australia. Looked suitably sad and said, 'what a shame, when they left. Put Jonah into tent number 11 the next night for a report on the fracas in the toilet but he heard only two sets of semi-silent footsteps and no talking, shouting, or piano playing.

I got two of the boys to come to the club but they walked out

half way through because we wouldn't let them soak the other kids. Sandy spent three hours cleaning what had been a brand new tent with all new equipment four days before.

However we did discover a new use for the children's club packs. When we asked for their club cards they said that they had been thrown away as the bag and contents had been used by the youngest, during the journey, as a sick bag.

Footnote: Had this mob been on the ferry that caught fire, they would have had it under control in seconds with their super soakers.

CHAPTER 13

Wild fire was not confined only to the breasts of Dan and Elulia. It also broke out on a ferry bringing some of our holiday— makers from Plymouth to Roscoff thereby causing alarm, despondency, fouled up schedules and singed clients.

It had been one of those weeks.

On Saturday the site had experienced a mad influx of caravans as the French poured in in a manner reminiscent of the mob who invaded the English countryside around Hastings in 1066. Instead of bows and arrows they were armed with radios and televisions which proved to be far more lethal and, had they then been available, King Harold would have finished up deaf as well as blind and dead.

Madam S and her minions dashed around the site followed by campers in cars as they directed people to their allotted sites, then rushed back for the next lot.

Springheel Jacques came into his own, driving round in J. C. s. vehicle and bawling through a megaphone to tell newcomers about treats he had organised for their entertainment. His trips complicated the already tangled traffic on the narrow roads as he always seemed to be travelling in the opposite direction to everyone else. A row of cars would be waiting while a caravan manoeuvred onto a plot, only to reveal him coming against the flow. With great authority and little comprehension he would scream distorted instructions through his megaphone that had cars and caravans backing into hedges, water pipes, electrical pillars, dustbins, and toilet blocks to the shouted annoyance of Hervé or Elulia who had to repair or rectify them.

A Courier's Reports are Never...

And the newcomers surged around in an unkempt tide as they sought out the facilities and broke through the hedges and fences in attempts to find short cuts. Bedlam reigned as the racket ran riot and tempers got shorter as the day got longer.

It brought out the best in Winston and his clients.

We listened through the hedge as he was besieged by a newly arrived family who found nowhere to park as all the plots around the tent were cluttered with cars, caravans, prams, cycles, tents, dogs, children, and people playing with bats, balls, racquets, shuttlecocks, frisbees and footballs. They would have had more success had they complained to the Health Authority that all the air was used up.

"Our plot's too small." snarled the man.

"What you want me to do, stretch it?" asked Winston.

"Less of your lip, young man." said the woman.

We could hear Winston glower.

"We want to move," said the man.

"Be my guest," invited Winston, "jump about."

"We want another tent."

"There isn't one."

"That plot is not big enough. It's misrepresented in the brochure".

"That plot is not illustrated in the brochure," replied Winston, now on firm ground.

"Right," said the man furiously, "we're going to sue you."

"Fat lot of good that'll do," Winston retorted, "I've got home made fags and holes in me socks. You can have them if you want."

We heard Minnie come out of the mobile.

"Oh, hello," she said brightly, "would you like to buy tickets for our aperitif party?"

They never seemed to have much luck with their ticket sales.

- O -

We didn't have much luck with the plot next to our courier tent.

We returned from shopping for our party to find that Madam S had let it to eight Dutch teenagers, and five tents had sprung up like mushrooms. The guy ropes of one were tied to our tent and another was partly under our outside table. I pointed this out to her.

"They camp there for a month every year." said she, then excused herself and, splashing sweat as she beetled off, left us aghast as the lads tested their stereo and ran up an old bra on their flagpole.

During the daytime the lads added to the general hullabaloo and during the night they created a hubbub all their own, keeping everyone in the vicinity awake until five a.m.

So at 10 in the morning I held our children's club meeting outside their tents until J. C. called the somulent teenagers to the office for an ultimatum at which I turned down the volume on our kids.

Volume was also belting from next door.

In time for the start of this annual French holiday, the building work finished on the adjacent campsite.

The clients in our tents had two day's respite before our neighbour`s campers arrived and found the acoustics in the new toilet block were perfect for "the Banana Boat Song", and other such choral arrangements. And as the echo there was most perfect between 2 a.m. and 5 a.m. it brought a rash of complaints from our high season clients.

"Is it always like this." shouted Mr. Bailey, as we stood by his tent with the toilet choir rendering, i.e. ripping to shreds, one of the movements from "La Traviata, and Springheel ground past in low gear yawping through his bullhorn.

"No," I yelled back, "it will get noisy in August."

Springheel spotted us and gave a special bellow our way. Mr. Bailey's 'kiss me quick hat` fell off. "Low grade sod," he screamed. "By the way, there are two babies in the next tent that cry all night."

"Point them towards the fence," I advised, "get your own back"

Edith soon spotted Mr. Bailey.

"I love men like that." she said.

"You love men like anything." I replied.

"Coo," she said, reading his hat, "I'm going to take advantage of that." She turned towards me; the sweat on her brow began to steam. "Do you think he'll be at the barbecue?"

"Yes," I said, having sold him a ticket, "but he's not on the menu."

Or so I thought.

A Courier's Reports are Never...

CHILDRENS COURIERS WEEKLY REPORT

Site Name: St. Armand   Date: 17th July

Couriers: Sandy and Peter   Numbers: +19

Venue on Site: Wherever provides nearby campers with the most annoyance.

Advertised Programme: Monday; Tomahawk run and games.

Wednesday; Beach Party. Friday; Scavenger Hunt.

General summary of week; Monday morning; eighteen children painted faces as Indians and had a tomahawk run around five wigwams thoughtfully provided on an adjacent plot, then loudly played guessing games.

Wednesday; combined with Heavenly for a beach party for 5 year old Louise.

Nineteen kids arrived and played games while I ate their crisps and sweets.

Friday; Went to the beach where we found a man scavenging amongst the high tide flotsam. The kids hunted him until he fled screaming into the sea. They sometimes seem to get the wrong angle on things.

Any incidents or comments

Little Ada Smith, aged five, has threatened to rape Michael Johnson, aged six, and we await the outcome with interest. Where do you get our clients from?

- O -

The barbecue was the first one organised by the site and so we couriers, being experienced in such matters, offered our services.

"No," said J. C., "it's all in hand; we've got a chef."

"There's a lot of difference," I pointed out, "between cooking on a range and barbecuing on a charcoal fire."

He smiled condescendingly. "A professional chef, he is. We only need you to sell tickets to your clients, and you can come free".

And with that he went off to half clean the pool while I completed a notice about the spate of blockades in which the French were indulging.

One of the French national pastimes is disruption.

During the winter they think of ways to disrupt the electrical and gas services thus helping the National debt by allowing old people to die of cold. In summer they disrupt travellers by having air traffic controllers go on strike thereby preventing any flights over their country.

A Courier's Reports are Never...

They also disrupt supplies of English beef by overturning lorries and supplies of English lamb by setting fire to them.

And the government helps where it can by thinking up ways to provoke their people into causing disruption, because the government is there for the people.

This year was no exception and the government had come up with a law whereby any driver who accumulated a certain number of offences would automatically be banned. This of course incensed the lorry drivers who declared that it discriminated against the professional, infringed his right to drive fast and recklessly, park dangerously and terrorise drivers of smaller vehicles.

And, in order to have the law changed into one in their favour, they disrupted the country by blockading the main roadways.

Television programmes were suddenly dominated by views of motorways clogged with lorries while endless queues of motorists backed up from Calais to Toulouse.

At first, nonchalant galoise smoking lorry drivers sneered at gesticulating policemen while indoor shots showed politicians pleading with intransigent union officials. These soon changed to speeches by the French President followed by programmes of arguing participants, followed by scenes of riot police, with shields and helmets, breaking windscreens and moving lorries.

Retaliation took the form of lorries travelling at one kilometre per hour in every motorway lane which meant that clients arrived with tempers frayed and tongues lashing.

"Why can't your route take account of blocked motorways?" a demented traveller screamed at Winston.

"If it did there'd be no point in me organising the fucking blockade in the first place." snarled Winston, who took everything personally.

SmartCamp Notice:

BLOCKADE

Talks between the French Government, the Drivers Union of Legal Lorries, D.U.L.L., and the Gallic Association of French Farmers, GAFF, have broken down and industrial action is continuing.

The situation has been worsened by DULL and GAFF being joined by FROG (French Organisation of Garlic Growers) and SWILL (Sewage Workers Industrial League).

All channel ports are expected to be blockaded by lorries, tractors, potatoes, garlic bread, onions, frogs' legs and effluent and the French police are giving stranded motorists gas masks, wellies & artificial resuscitation.

It is anticipated that the situation will ease by Christmas but all Mucus and Heavenly clients should report to their couriers every twenty minutes for the latest information.

Arrangements have been made for Smartcamp clients to return to England on Concarneau fishing boats. A small extra cost is involved and passengers will be expected to assist in cutting other trawlers nets, throwing belaying pins and shouting English insults.

On their day of departure, Smartcamp clients should hand a cash cheque for £150 to their couriers and report to the harbour master at Concarneau who will tell them where to go.

A Courier's Reports are Never...

Surprisingly, none of his Winston's clients went to the barbecue.

It was advertised to start at seven p.m. with drinks of cardboard wine. As we were not needed, we ran reception as usual and I put up a notice telling clients of our dire circumstances because a) our previous notice was not fooling enough suckers and b) idiot clients with nothing better to do than ponder on us kept asking questions about our backgrounds.

"What did you do in real life?" and "what do you do during the winter?" were cries most frequently heard. So I published a bunch of lies to keep them guessing, collected Sandy, Winston, Minnie, Edith and Cindy Birdsong and we made our way to the revelry.

And found it as flat as yesterdays pancake.

Customers sat around in disgruntled array, scowling at one another and pulling faces at the wine. They slumped sullenly against long trestle tables while in the background Madam S, J. C. and assorted helpers frantically threw matches onto charcoal heaped in halved oil drums, sweated and called on the gods for help. And the gods, disguised as couriers, arrived to answer the call.

I nipped off for bottles of barbecue fluid, petrol and Edith's cologne with which to ignite the reluctant coals while Sandy, Winston and Minnie broke open packs of sausages, pork chops, beef and lamb and sprinkled them with seasoning.

Cindy, being versed in entertaining junior minds, leapt onto the tables, waived herself around and led the punters in community singing whilst Edith passed amongst them, groping and encouraging.

And the chef, seeing the proceedings light up in counterpoint to the way his fires wouldn't, beat time with the bottle from which he was drinking and joined in the singing. The fact that he was singing "Frère Jacques" in contrast to our "over the mountain, caused him not a moment's dismay and he set to with a will.

Madam S however was dismayed to see the latest in a long line of quality chefs adhering to tradition and becoming pissed in public so she approached him and spoke as follows: "Stop it, stop it. Get this food cooked at once."

The chef seemed not to hear, continued singing and beat time with his bottle on a passing reveller. But the reveller, having spent the previous day burning out his clutch as he drove from Paris to Brittany behind a dawdling lorry, was in no mood to humour drunken French chef's so he removed the bottle and brained the chef with it.

"Serve him right." said Madam S, as the chef slumped in a heap at her feet; the punters began to sing "The Red Flag" in honour of Bastille Day, and she shoved off to keep a maternal eye on Jean-Claud as he struggled with a half-cooked sausage.

A Courier's Reports are Never...

But we couriers persevered and the air was filled with the pervading smell of perfectly cooked meat and the sounds of salivating campers as they queued for their portions.

And soon the chomp and burp of contented noshers overlaid the snores of the chef and all was repleated peace, serenity and a desire to move to the next item on the agenda.

Which was disco music.

What, we did know was that the musicians had not arrived; what we didn't know was that they were stuck in a blockade and wouldn't be coming.

Madam S, having already experienced such vibes from the crowd, recognised a return of their ugly mood, wrung her hands and again spoke as follows: "What shall we do? Oh, what shall we do?"

But Elulia hadn't been a flower person for nothing ; not only had she sat around sniffing blooms and thinking sweet thoughts, she had passed idle moments in playing a guitar and busy moments plugged into a radio, which gave her the ability to pluck a tune and a knowledge of all the latest hits.

So she nipped off to the converted brick coal store without wheels that was now home, unchained the new metal door, and galloped back waiving her guitar and Hervé's accordion.

Then, accompanied on the washboard by a recently revived chef, they broke into an impromptu arrangement of, "if you should go to San Francisco," followed by a duo playing of "Twelfth Street Rag." with a washboard accompaniment of "Freré Jaques."

And all was happiness for a while but the musical attention span of the average camper is limited and the audience soon began to shuffle as a restless mood took their feet; and belch as the unaccustomed diet reached their stomachs, and they become uncomfortable and unsettled.

So I grabbed Cindy Birdsong and leapt onto the vacant space in front of the Elulia/Hervé/Boozer trio and we oscillated before the appreciative audience.

What has not previously been mentioned was that Cindy Birdsong had long swinging fair hair and a nubile figure around which clothes seemed to flow and hug. And never more so than when contorting her body to the strains of modern music.

To a man the audience looked and drooled and to a woman it watched and envied.

Which was too much for Edith who preferred to be at the centre.

So, snatching Mr. Bailey from where he was standing draped under his wife's arm, she dragged him onto the dance floor and began her speciality which was a form of rape done to music and would have brought a frowning 'tut tut, now now` from the most liberal of film censors had it been entered for a rating; in fact it would never have received a certificate of even 21 or over, and stood a vague chance of being awarded an 'over 80 provided they are impotent.'

And Mr. Bailey's woman, being his common law wife and therefore not legally bound, began to seethe at this threat to her security as the evening throbbed on with passions rising and libidos being released.

Winston and Minnie joined in with a type of Adagio dance during which he slung her about, Edith worked on perfecting her style and seducing Mr. Bailey, Sandy ricocheted about with the assistant barman, the Alsatian howled, and Hervé and Elulia sweated, played, watched each other laughingly and got in tune.

It was after a particularly frenzied number, as they stood close, chortling and, with their eyes, promising each other a tremendous finale that we became aware of a disturbance at the edge of the crowd.

And, as the disturbance came closer and moved onto the spot lit stage, we saw that it was Dan forcing spectators aside as he thrust forwards to retrieve his loved one. And following in his wake with the same intention was Mrs. Bailey.

Hervé gave a terrified squeal on his accordion and smashed his way through a nearby drink laden table with Dan in close pursuit, as Mrs. Bailey reached her fingers into Edith's locks and pulled, and the chef, spotting his former assailant, brought the washboard down on his head.

It is better to draw a veil over the ensuing carnage as campers took sides and joined in.

Sufficient to say that we courier's were never invited to another site barbecue and our concerted opinion was that Madam S would have preferred that the riot commence earlier caused by lack of food, as she would then have saved the cost of feeding the savages and still reaped the same end result.

And I privately thought that Jean-Claud, instead of using professional help, would rather have stuck to his usual practice and had a half finished barbecue.

But even the most accomplished couriers can't please them all.

- O -

SMARTCAMP HOLIDAYS

Couriers Weekly Report

Site Name: St. Armand   Report N°: 8

Couriers: Peter and Sandy

Week Ending: 17th July

(Summarise your week including details of Weather, Site and Client Problems, Facilities

A Courier's Reports are Never...

and Competitors)

Saturday brought an influx of French campers. Over 100 units arrived and the site staff rushed around like guillotined chickens.

With experience they may get their act together in a few years time. Or perhaps it was a practice for Bastille Day which the site celebrated on Wednesday with a barbecue. Some of our clients attended and the couriers were told that they could go for no charge and, because of site expertise, all was in hand and our aid was not required. However being kind of heart and thick of skin, we couriers all climbed in and helped; a necessity as the chef, in the best traditions of his predecessors, got himself drunk which resulted in dismissal and no one to process the nosh.

So we helped out and the campers seemed to thoroughly enjoy the evening and really let themselves go.

The site now has a new chef; a morose individual who looks like a bald, smooth-topped fruitcake and is miserable enough to be a member of Alcoholics Anonymous. He has not been introduced to us as chefs do not last long enough for us to take the trouble to learn their names; or perhaps he is an alcoholic and wishes to remain anonymous.

Tuesday brought us Mrs. Crouch from whom I expected trouble as she wanted a shady, open site with mini-tent and manicured grass.

She was all I could hope for and within one hour her husband was pressing for a transfer as she is claustrophobic and depressed by trees. I pointed her at Douarnenez and Pont l` Abbot so she rushed around visiting, then turned them down because her two girls are happy on this site. We have been cultivating her and she now eats crisps and nuts from my hand, and came to our aperitif party. I think she has been won over.

Mrs. Tallons, was even more insidious that I thought. To the last she tried to subvert our clients and should be either black listed or put down.

Saturday, sunday and monday were showery, rainy or downright wet, their only use being to water the drooping shrubs and drive Mr. and Mrs. Yukkie and their four soggy sons back into the oblivion of Berwick on Tweed. In a sudden spurt of relief at their leaving, the sun came out and has been blazing hot ever since.

Eight Dutch teenagers, sprouting from five tents were placed on the next plot to our courier tent. They have loud voices, louder radios, and constant repartee with passing females. On their first night they stayed up carousing until 5am. and were reprimanded by the site owners for this. Now they are more silent at night, taking their boisterousness to the beach until each 4am. But, in the day-time they are musical and highly vocal and I don't envy the Heavenly clients next to and opposite, who came here presumably for a quiet family holiday.

Friday brought a lack of two clients' families who were drifting helplessly on a smoke filled ferry half way between Plymouth and Roscoff, eating free food and frying gently in the noonday sun. The couriers organised a watching schedule throughout the night and the clients, with families complete, arrived at 6am. in time for next week's report. I asked their children which of them started the fire but, although they deny it, their conduct at children's Club makes them highly suspect.

CHAPTER 14

We heard about the ferry on fire late on Friday evening.

The clients ensconced on it should have arrived during the afternoon instead of which they were up aloft, warming their heads in the blazing sun and their feet on the heated deck, as fire raged below and, those who could swim, wondered how far it was to the nearest shore.

But this was unbeknown to us as we paced about and cursed the thoughtlessness of clients who failed to arrive when expected.

Until Edith and ourselves received word from our English offices about the fire, instructing us to hang about until our charred and traumatised clients should appear, if and whenever that might be.

The only criticism Winston had of his firm, apart from its habit of sending him clients, was that his computer print out never indicated by which ferry his punters would arrive.

So when ten o' clock came with three clients missing, he hoped for the best and went to bed, knowing that his action, or lack of it, would be supported by Rupert whose motto of 'let the buyer beware` was so well entrenched that it had been plagiarised by English law.

Meanwhile Sandy, Edith and myself took turns at watching and sleeping while lorry drivers dozed by their blockades waiting to add their welcome to our ferry victims.

But our sleep was fitful with concern and morning found us up early, somewhat drained and draining in turn numerous cups of coffee.

Our fatigue gave us empathy with our clients when they arrived, glassy eyed, at 9am.

We passed them well-percolated coffee and sympathy as they gave out tales of rushing up on deck, being separated from loved ones in the crush, listening to explosions down below and wondering how to lower the lifeboats.

They told of how helicopters quickly arrived to hover overhead, how ships later came to circle round and how their ferry drifted helplessly until tugs appeared to tow them onwards into Roscoff.

And for thirty hours they had to stay up on deck while the sun scorched down, and the food ran low and the toilets overflowed.

And then they drove their weary selves through the blurring French countryside to our site, where we tenderly led them to their mobiles, soothed then and put them to bed.

And on the way back I found three couples with assorted crying children besieging the Heavenly reception.

"All right, all right," snapped a tousled Winston, appearing suddenly like a demon king, "don't knock the fucking door down."

"We've been stuck on a ferry," sobbed a woman, sorely in need of soothing sympathy, sleep and sustenance.

In spite of himself it struck a note of interest in Winston.

"What," he asked, "jammed in the gangway or something."

"No, the ferry caught fire."

"Did it?" he said, amazed, "Well blow me. That's a right giggle, isn't it?"

"It wasn't funny." snapped the sobbing one's husband.

"Why? Did you have to swim for it?"

"No. Look, just show us to our mobiles, will you ?"

"Yehr, 0 K." he said, fetching the keys, then unbending somewhat said "Hope you don't get the same one going back."

"Oh, god." said the woman.

- O -

We were becoming adept at running children's club and could now do it with our eyes closed, which was fortunate as seventeen of the swine turned up for the 10am. meeting.

Zombie like from our night's vigil we staggered amongst them pandering to their junior minds.

Sandy had fortunately prepared, during the night's waking hours, a board pasted with photos of well known personalities on which we quizzed them.

But this lot's television intake was limited mainly to dinosaurs and cartoon characters, so the only ones they got right were President Bush and John Major. Excepting of course cardboard people from current soap operas about which they demonstrated amazing knowledge.

"That's Emily who's married to Jed but had a baby by Tom who was engaged to Charlotte until she got pregnant after a gangbang with the Luton Boys Choir" said little Zoë, aged six.

A Courier's Reports are Never...

The rest nodded sagely in engrossed agreement.

"She was lonely," Wee Jimmy excused her conduct, "because Jed was inside after being picked up as a pusher during a drugs bust."

"His own fault," opinioned another tiny developing mite, "if he hadn't been a right wimp and had knifed that copper he could have escaped through the brothel window."

"I would've," said Gregory, a small pug-nosed kid who was inappropriately dressed in pink dungarees embroidered with bunny rabbits, "I'd have wasted the pig."

Sandy and I looked at one another.

"Who's this?" she put in quickly to stop the flow.

"How would I know?" asked Zoe, contemplating a photo of the Pope, "unless he's the vicar who married Michael and Jeremy at that gay wedding."

We tried to divert them with paper and crayons so as to have drawings with which to decorate the tent but, as their favourite characters were uppermost in their minds, these turned out to be badly drawn but recognisable pictures of a heavily pregnant Charlotte or Jed carving pieces off a policeman.

And when they began to imitate their favourites and get destructive, we took them to the basketball pitch where they could vent their talents in the fresh air.

And hoped that we would be far away when they grew up.

- O -

CHILDRENS COURIERS WEEKLY REPORT

Site Name: St. Armand   Date: 24th July

Couriers: Sandy and Peter   Numbers: Varies up to 17 max.

Venue on Site: Under camper's feet

Advertised Programme: Saturday; Personality Quiz. Tuesday: Boules Competition. Tues. Evening; Scavenger Hunt. Thursday;

Beach Games.

General Summary of Week: Seventeen little rotters arrived and showed their abysmal ignorance of well-known personalities.

Drew drawings afterwards until they got boisterous, then wore them out with basketball, karate and chloroform.

Tuesday; 7 kids turned up and wreaked havoc on the boules pitch as usual.

Tuesday evening; 12 drunken children scoured the campsite after topping-up at the aperitif party.

Thursday; 9 of ours beat the hell out of the Heavenly gang on the beach after which we collected cockles. However we will not play against Heavenly in future as we are running low on bandages.

Any incidents or comments

Leah Porridge, on arrival, began puking due, we think, to a surfeit of sun the previous day. Took her back to her parents where they, at breakfast, were treated to a vomiting display.

- O -

At times a courier longs to be far away.

He dreams of an uninhabited island well away from marauding clients and other savages, where the only caller is the postman dropping in every three years to tell him he has won the football pools yet again.

But his reality is hordes of clients, each with it's own petty problems, and each demanding priority.

Our problems were intensified by lack of sleep due to waiting up until the early hours for former Roscoff arrivees now being re-routed through other ports.

And the clients were angry because they had taken the trouble to programme their trip via a port one hour from the site and their alternative ports gave them a journey of between four and eight hours.

And, naturally, they blamed their courier for this.

"What do you think you're doing?" a client yelled at Winston as he arrived from Cherbourg.

He had suffered because his long drive was compounded by phase four of the blockade controversy.

Due to a combination of police wrecking lorries by pushing them off motorway embankments, and drivers' leaders negotiating with government agents, the blockade was officially over.

However farmers, incensed by their produce being left to rot, while the drivers had their fun, felt it now their turn and emptied their unusable fruit and veg over main roads thus effectively preventing the lorry drivers passing and making up lost earnings.

And the farmers underlined their displeasure by driving tractors slowly along any motorway that their produce had failed to render impassable.

"I've been held up by a motorway covered with potatoes." shouted Winston's

A Courier's Reports are Never...

Cherbourg client.

Winston was unmoved by the man's dilemma. "Did you pick up a few spuds for me?" he asked.

The man danced about as only a Heavenly client could.

"I booked through Roscoff," he yorped, "and you changed it."

"We had to, didn't we?" answered Winston, beginning to get as heated as a ferry.

"I wouldn't have had this trouble if you'd kept to my original booking. How did the fire start anyway?"

"I went out in a rowboat and put a match to it just to fuck you about." snarled Winston.

Our clients, arriving after a longer drive than anticipated, were more malleable due to our smothering them in soft soap and being older.

Oily smarm worked wonders and they followed us gratefully to their accommodation in a mesmerised manner.

Except Mrs. Watts.

The DAILY NEWS

Monday 26th July 1992   20p

YELTSIN TO BORROW £6 BILLION

A delighted President Yeltsin was today handed a cheque for £6 billion in an informal ceremony to mark the end of communism in Russia and a return to the free market capitalist system.

'The money will be spent wisely and will rescue my people from the famine which threatens,' said a smiling Boris Yeltsin. 'Without this loan all my efforts could have dissolved in counter revolution.' He then went on to express his relief, and gratitude to Smartcamp for the loan.

In reply a nonchalant Fred Smart-Camp, owner and president of the company, said. 'Peanuts, boy; its small change to an organisation like ours and besides us presidents gotta stick together.' When asked if there was any ulterior motive in granting the loan Mr. Smart-Camp responded, 'of course there bloody is.' What do you think we are, a charity?

Yeltsin signals victory.

We pay our couriers lousy so we can make a boodle for development and now we got our foot in the door.'

Asked to explain he elucidated, 'What's to explain? Them Ruskies got camps in Siberia ideal for the types of client we attract. We don't even have to put in watch-towers or barbed wire and they got dungeons perfect for the activity couriers, and salt mines for the children's club, so what's to explain, you berk?'

A Courier's Reports are Never...

Mrs. Watts returned to reception after perusing her surroundings for five minutes, read my notice about Yeltsin, and snorted.

"That tent eleven's disgusting." she said.

I cast my mind back.

I had helped Sandy cart all the innard outside after Mr. Yukkie and his contamination team had pulled out, and she had scoured it for three hours. I knew that the smell had dispersed and I couldn't see a problem.

"Why?" I asked.

"All those . . . ." she thought deeply, "rows of . . . , er. My children can see straight along the urinals."

"Turn your children the other way."

"We want to move." she said, unimpressed by logic.

Two days before we had had two calls from a Mr. Brown.

The first at 8pm. said he would be late; the second at 10p.m. said he would be later. At 2a.m. we gave up and went to bed. The next day he failed to arrive. He was my favourite client.

So I transferred Mrs. Watts to Mr. Brown's tent number 4 and reprogrammed him adjacent to the shithouse where he belonged.

She was most grateful. "I am most grateful." she said, and allowed her kids to cry all night in tent n°. 4 in the middle of our enclave, which brought a rash of complaints from the others.

"She's Fred Smart-Camp's daughter." I told them, and so they bought her burping syrup and shut up.

Mr. Kindlewood didn't shut up even though he, with wife and two little girls, arrived a day late and expressed sorrow that we had waited up.

He approached me the next day as I relaxed, in flagged out torpor by our courier tent, off duty in shorts and tan.

"I'm sorry to bother you." he lied.

I could see he wasn't. Having waited up until 2 a.m. for clients and risen at 6 a.m. to give departures an early call and make sure we got rid of them, I was in no mood for gossip in my free time. "There's a big problem," he waived an arm, "near the pool."

"A client drowning." I said hopefully, but he shook his head.

"Come and see."

A Courier's Reports are Never...

So I dragged to my feet and he led me to the Jacuzzi.

"There." he said.

I failed to see.

"Have a close look." he said.

I went into the enclosure and looked closely. He shook his head in an exasperated manner as a crowd began to form.

"It's a poor frog," he explained, "been there for two days. It'll drown."

So I carefully picked it out, to the applause of the onlookers, took it round the corner and dropped it in the dust bin.

Your courier can get nasty when roused.

- O -

SMARTCAMP HOLIDAYS

Couriers Weekly Report

Site Name: St. Armand   Report N°: 9

Couriers: Peter and sandy

Week Ending: 24th July

(Summarise your week including details of Weather, Site and Client Problems, Facilities and Competitors)

Our all-night vigil for smoke dried ferry victims proved useful in that it adapted us to sleeplessness, as re-routed clients now appear via Cherbourg from between 11 p.m. and 1 a.m. depending on their navigational prowess. The site owners, in a spasm of understanding, leave the barrier open until early morning which eases the trek between somulent caravans. We waited up until 2 a.m. for Mr. Kindlewood, who arrived a day late bemused because he had faxed the London Office asking that you inform us that he would stay overnight in a hotel. In view of this, if a client has not arrived within two hours of the anticipated time, we will take to our beds and, if he happens to turn up, he must find us.

Mr. Holden and Mr. Wicks, our ferry wrecked clients, have now recovered from their lack of sleep and sun-blistered state and are enjoying themselves, each in his own individual way; one quietly and one with merry jests, but each has shown his trauma by removing the battery from the mobiles" smoke detectors.

Dr. McFussy arrived after dark and stated that this campsite is not as good as Perros. He must have X-ray vision although he did admit when he left that this is an excellent campsite and he may have been a little hasty. I hope his diagnoses on his patients are more considered and accurate. Regarding his list of comments; we had 4 children's club meetings during his 6 days and he sent his kids to only 2 of them. He was the only person who did not attend the aperitif party. "Fifteen francs each fa ma bairns, he said, 'at`s awfu dear."

The aperitif party was enjoyed and no drunks fell in alcoholic stupor across the drinks table, showing the quality of our clients.

After a showery Friday and Saturday the weather got progressively more hot and sunny, leaving a trail of happy blistered clients and a pervading smell of calamine and after-sun that defeats the estuary ozone. All is cheery bonhomie, broken by the occasional grizzle from a re-routed Roscoff traveller as he chaffs at the extra mileage. So I tell them to claim reimbursement for any out-of-pocket costs from the port of departure and leave them happily calculating extra layout to the last litre. McFussy wants to claim for a hotel at the port of entry and said he would be set back in his travels by 12 hours. He will probably try to claim expenses on an hourly rate for doctors and good luck to him.

CHAPTER 15

Some clients are nasty even when not roused.

"Where were you?" growled a vague shape as it shone a torch on me at 1.30 in the morning.

I knew it was not roused as it had not yet been to bed.

This was our first introduction to The Unutterably Foul.

Until that enchanting moment, Mr. Kindlewood had been the fly that most often shoved its feet into our ointment.

He hovered constantly, darting in to settle on us for a quick word or buzzing round then nipping off and back before we could swat him. He crawled all over us and got up our noses.

I tried to envelope him in Edith's web.

"You say he's a very nice bloke." she said, regarding him doubtfully.

Although of middle age, he was tall, slim, wavy-haired and clean-cut. She preferred them short, dark, hairy and mucky. But what the hell; it was a man, wasn't it?

"You're a real man." she said, netting him as he buzzed past.

He blinked, never having been told that before.

A Courier's Reports are Never...

"Oh yes," she continued, "a real male."

He tore himself away.

"I'll put you on my mailing list," she called as he zoomed in on us.

She put many clients on the list, but we were not sure if it was her's or her firm's.

Although, at all times, Kindlewood treated us like particularly tasty dustbins, he was at his most insidious during children's club. He must have been the most doting parent ever.

We never saw Mrs. Kindlewood but his solitary doting more than made up for her.

Of an advanced age for the father of such young girls, never likely to reproduce further, he demonstrated how closely related are dotage and doting.

His two small girls were used to his prowling and secreting himself with a camera, rather as royalty accepts constant exposure to the reporters' lens.

As the Kids Club perambulated through the campsite, he could be discovered burrowing beneath a car or dangling from a tree branch to obtain the unexpected angle shot. We became expert at determining his whereabouts by noting the angle of his daughters' heads as they presented their best profiles.

From a petulant riposte at another child, they would suddenly blossom.

A pretty pucker to the mouth, a half smile, a widening of the eyes would tell us that we were about to hear a shutter click.

At first the other kids were bemused by the transformation but soon learnt its cause and joined in. From being a shambling mob, tossing toads through windows, releasing air from tyres, kicking stones at dogs, they would suddenly jerk alert, become orderly, and assume photogenic expressions.

It was quite disconcerting but we had to admit that the sudden glint of sunlight on Kindlewood's sniper lens had a beneficial effect on discipline.

But to have him crawling, climbing and flitting around us was extremely wearing. One can't really chastise kids effectively if one is likely to be exposed on film.

He was particularly intrusive and unwelcome at the Monday's kids club as we were trying out a new wheeze of Sandy's. Instead of spending ages preparing a quiz or cutting out and pasting peoples' photos' on cards she came up with an idea whilst watching me top up our fuel tank at the local self-service garage.

"They can do it themselves." she said.

"Huh?" I replied.

So at the next kids club, she put her scheme into operation.

A Courier's Reports are Never...

She sent half the kids one way to compile a list of questions and half the other way to ditto while we basked outside reception. Then, at half time, she swapped the lists and we basked some more while the kids sweated around finding out the other team's answers. And, being evil, the kids were out to thwart their opponents with difficult questions.

"How many washbasin taps are there on the campsite?" asked the perspiring leader of team A.

"Go and count them," said Sandy, nonchalantly blowing cigarette smoke at him and slumping back into the chair with her coffee cup.

Kindlewood flitted up as the team dashed of. "You should be supervising them." he said, as it added content to his pictures to have us in the background.

"Initiative," I replied, "We are trained to develop initiative and self reliance in the kiddiewinkies."

"Yes but supposing…"

"Supposing you meet Edith," I said, waving her across, "who is the ultimate in initiative…."

"What's wrong with him." Edith asked as we watched him flee.

"I told him you would show him the difference between a wasp and a fly." I said.

"What is the difference?" she asked.   I watched our pest zoom out of sight.

"You can't unzip a wasp." I said.

Your courier is versed in using natural resources.

- O -

CHILDRENS COURIERS WEEKLY REPORTS

Site Name: St. Armand   Date: 31st July

Couriers: Sandy and Peter   Numbers: 16 to 33

Venue on Site: Far and Wide

Advertised Programme: Monday; Campsite Quiz. Wednesday: Beach Hunt. Thursday; Craft and Painting. Friday Eve; String hunt.

General summary of week: Monday; divided seventeen kids into two teams and sent them off to compile 25 questions about the campsite. Then they swapped questions and searched out the answers. They were enthusiastic and took up more than the two hours. Wednesday; first, item on the hunt was a crab. The fascination of hooking them with a barnacle on the end of a fishing line hooked the kids and became a competition to see

117

who could catch the most. Thursday; by unanimous vote tinged with mutiny, we had to go back and catch crabs again. This is so addictive that, out of club hours, the kids take their parents and hook crabs. The crabs are always released in a crab race back to the sea and are becoming shy and learning not to dive on barnacles suspended on fishing lines. CONCLUSION: the crabs are more intelligent than the kids.

Friday; had no time to organise the string hunt as friday was a busy, fouled up, problem filled day. So we had a scavenger hunt, instead. This was at the aperitif party but afterwards the kids, noting that mutiny works, forced me to take them playing cricket, on the beach until it got too dark. Sandy cleared away and washed up after the party and I think she had the best deal.

Any incidents or comments

Little Sophie Morton was hit on the nose by a cricket ball during the beach game and cried when it bled. However she laughed when she got home and proudly showed her mother what a pretty pattern the blood had made on her dress. These kids are tough.

Mr. Kindlewood, our current posterior pain, complained on Monday, when he noticed that one team had 9 members and the other only 8, that the teams were unequal thus giving one an unfair advantage. As he was concerned and serious in his comment, I promised to have one of the children culled.

- O -

As I took the Unutterably Foul back to reception to book it in, I reflected on how pleasant it had all been until now; rather in the way that someone's post life flashes by when at death's door.

The Tallons, compared to this object, were happy benign people.

McFussy suddenly became desirable, Bickerstaff a bundle of delight. I longed for the enjoyable vapid conversation of Yukkie as we discussed the effect of wet rot on puberty.

And shuddered at this thing enveloping me in the night's gloom.

We had become too complaisant, something your professional courier has to be wary of.

Shipwreck Wicks had cheered up as scabs formed over his sun- baked scalp and prevented further blistering; had even volunteered his address for Edith's list, not realising that she would pass part of her off-season as his guest.

Which shows that being rescued from a watery grave can leave a residue of water on the brain.

Castaway Holden had stopped jibbering whenever something popped near him although he still refused to light his barbecue.

A Courier's Reports are Never...

Mrs. Watts talked loudly and guiltily over her children's crying to show it wasn't happening.

We had installed a Mr. Alien and family in the tent in the corner of the enclave and his shy, polite and effacing ways added to our unwary state. And then The Unutterably arrived.

The DAILY NEWS

Monday 2nd August 1992   20p

OLYMPICS

The Olympic Games opened in Barcelona with a march past of thousands of athletes from all countries of the world. The impressive ceremony was highlighted by the release of 20,000 doves and culminated in the lighting of the Olympic Flame.

In his opening address in the packed royal stadium, Fred Smart-Camp owner of Smartcamp and Vice-president of the games commented, 'I want to thank my pal King Juan Carlos and all his dago mates for letting us hold the games in his country. Mind you, it's a nice little earner for him what with all the tourists it brings in.

He then continued with a history of the games and its value in uniting the world of sportsmen. 'It brings together all them wops, frogs and chinks in friendly rivalry instead of them ripping out each other's throats like they used to,' he commented.

He then accepted the Olympic torch which had been brought from Greece by a relay of Smartcamp activity couriers, lit his cigar from it and nonchalantly tossed it in the flame bowl to approving roars from the crowd.

At a subsequent cocktail party when asked how he saw the future of the Olympic village he stated that he might buy it as a Holiday Centre. Especially if they leave some of them nubile young female athletes behind,' he chuckled, 'make good couriers, they would, and then they'd be for the high jump.'

When asked if his good-fellowship extended to other companies such as Mucus and Heavenly he snarled, 'wash your mouth out, boy, and don't play games with me.'

A Courier's Reports are Never...

Frittering away the waiting moments, I wrote a notice to inform our clients about the opening of the Olympic Games and Sandy chatted to Elulia.

"Dan's mother doesn't know we're separated," she said, "and it's her eightieth birthday in ten day's time."

Elulia had developed the habit of confiding in Sandy as we waited up for the constant stream of late, diverted arrivals.

She now gazed into the dark night and thought dark thoughts.

"I want to spend the birthday with her in England if the swine will let me".

"Dan's not so bad", said Sandy.

"I'm talking about Madam S."

"Go and ask her." suggested Sandy, but Elulia's reply was drowned by screaming engines as vehicles rocketed through the entrance.

We listened to them hunting around the site, headlights piercing the night like searchlights until eventually the engines stopped and all was quiet.

"Thoughtless sods," I opinioned tolerantly, "it's one thirty."

"That last vehicle had a Smartcamp sticker." said Sandy.

"But our accommodation's the other way."

"Better go and see." she said, being very free with my energy, "it might be the Fowler mob."

So I galloped unsuspectingly off and came face to face with the horror that was the Unutterably Foul.

– O –

SMARTCAMP HOLIDAYS

Couriers Weekly Report

Site Name: St. Armand   Report N°: 10

Couriers: Peter and Sandy

Week Ending: 31st July

(Summary of your week including details of Weather, Site and Client Problems,

Facilities and Competitors)

In spite of our intent to let simple minded clients who, unable to read simple

A Courier's Reports are Never...

directions and arrive from Cherbourg via Paris, Lyon, Toulouse and Bordeaux, flounder around the campsite in the early hours crowing 'Smartcamp' like a pre-dawn chorus, our better natures, of which we have a surfeit, prevail and we pace the still hours, flashlight in hand, calling their names. Thus we came across the Unwin/Utterly/Fowler families who travel in convoy, and wish we hadn't. Families who request adjacent accommodation can be painful and exclude those around them. Three units together tend to take over by their sheer weight of numbers. This mob of indistinguishable people, known by only one name – The Unutterably Foul — was the ultimate in exclusive togetherness. Their kids volleyed, raquetted and cycled throughout the previously quiet Smartcamp tent enclave, while the parents pranced, paraded, shouted and showed their embryo hooligans how it should be done. We found the Alien family cowering in tent number eight, cut off from civilisation by this heaving mass, and they pleaded for a transfer to more salubrious parts. So we put them into tent number eleven, next to the toilet block, where they found the comparative silence of screaming, abluting campers far more serene. Tent eleven had previously been turned down as unsuitable by Mrs. Watts who prefers to teach her children sex education by more subtle means than having them exposed to men utilising the typical French urinals, and we had put her family into the tent previously earmarked for Mr. Brown who, after two phone calls to say he would be late, never arrived and is probably still on the Paris/ Lyon/ Toulouse/ Bordeaux circuit, or may even be stuck in a blockade of lorry drivers who don't yet know it is over.

Our next client, Mr. Trite, proved to be a self-contained, unimaginative man with a boat, so we shoved him into tent number eight on the premise that he wouldn't notice the bedlam by his front door, and Unutterably Foul would cultivate him in order to borrow his boat, and thus extend it's repertoire to include piracy. However Unutterably was quite content to utilise only the Smartcamp windsurfer in order to decimate the estuary, and our clients continued to wrangle over whose turn it was to use it, pitch about into the estuary mud and improve complexions. A week of blazing sun gave way on Friday to the odd shower to make our guests at the Aperitif Party feel at home. We had a convivial time due mainly to our inspiration of giving Unutterably a pamphlet showing the weeks highlights at Concarneau and translating the "Festival of the Blue Nets" to read "Blue Film Festival". He lustfully hurtled off to add pornography to his list of French Experiences, thus ensuring that our supply of Kir Royale was not seriously depleted in the first five minutes.

Our clients are running a competition to see who can forget the most luggage. They not only leave their brains at home, (an observation made by the Heavenly courier), but leave their belongings here on departure. Fortunately they have all remembered so far to take their children, as retrieval of livestock is not catered for in our instruction manual.

CHAPTER 16

August hit us with such noise and force that what had gone before was, in comparison, a lullaby.

On the first Saturday hundreds of campers surged in, reminiscent of the hordes that accompanied Gengis Khan on his jaunts except that these were louder and not so nice.

Like locusts they clogged every available space, even filling small plots on each side of the entrance road from which they released children to dodge out from behind cars, which partially blocked the road, then screamed at passing motorists as though their kids were not heavily insured.

The eight Dutch lads, with whom we had become friendly, added tone to the commotion by installing a speaker behind a group of garden gnomes at the front of their plot. The Heavenly clients nearby added their contribution by shouting at the Dutch lads. Unutterably Foul did it's bit with raucous racing between the pool complex and our tent enclave, which had now been turned by his screaming ricocheting offspring into a treacherous sea of mud about which he complained.

"It's slippery and dangerous; ought to be concreted." he said, being used to back alleys and having no eye for the beauty of nature.

So I introduced Unutterably to Edith whom he grouped around and groped whenever the female of whatever species he represented was not about; a further demonstration of his lack of appreciation of natural beauty.

"What nice people," she exclaimed, as they left her flushed and panting, "definitely on my mailing list. I'd like them in one of my mobiles."

She looked at me in an accusing manner, "Did you know that my mobiles are cheaper than your tents?"

"Yes," I said, "but our tents don't leak."

And leaking through the site was the pervading smell of overworked toilets.

Even Unutterably noticed it. "What's that bleeding stench?" he asked.

"Ozone." I said.

"Ozone," he mused, "that's a tree, enit?'

The quality of our expensive high season clients never failed to amaze me.

Amazing everybody with his incomprehensible announcements was Springheel Jacques.

Still weaving his way through traffic jams he had caused, he now screamed his wares into a microphone which led to a speaker fixed to the bonnet of the vehicle. His blurred

123

resonating screech was enhanced by speaker feedback as he raised the volume to full in an effort to drown out the competition from the animateur next door. They both assumed that volume not quality was the proof of who was better as they roared around their respective sites and the campers understood not a word. Even the French campers were baffled but they could at least read the notices.

Arriving clients would either quail at the tumult or smile and roll up their sleeves, depending on what they expected from a holiday, but fortunately most of ours arrived during the comparatively peaceful night hours.

But the peace of the night hours was always interrupted as Unutterably invariably returned after the barrier was down and inventively found ways to circumvent it, from picking the lock to hauling the barrier post down with a towrope.

This led to the frantic over-harassed owners employing an outside security service, and these black uniformed yobs would occasionally hurtle round the dark site with searchlights on their vehicles playing them onto tents and mobiles to wake the sleeping campers, thereby proving that they were up to the job.

The Heavenly clients naturally added this to the list of complaints that they gave Winston for onward transmission to the overworked owners, and even his arriving clients sensed that somewhere there was a Heavenly Complaints Club and applied for membership.

"Who do we complain to?" asked a client, stepping from his car.

"But you've only just arrived." protested Winston.

"Yes, but we're bound to have a complaint soon." responded the wife, sniffing the air.

"We want to borrow the swing ball, mum." put in their junior bellyacher.

"We don't have one." said Winston.

"But Smartcamp do." insisted the woman, who had travelled with us the previous year.

"But we don't."

"What about bats and balls?"

"We don't have any."

"Well there you are then," she said triumphantly, "that's our first complaint."

- O -

"They didn't want me to go." complained Elulia.

"What happened?" asked Sandy.

A Courier's Reports are Never…

Elulia had plucked up courage and cornered Madam S in reception as she panted in after depositing a new client amongst the chaos of her site. Jean-Claud stood in the background unruffled, not understanding the frenzied haste erupting around him.

In an uncommon respite before another client burst in Elulia spoke.

"It's my mother-in-law's birthday next week."

Madam S who had no time for tittle-tattle and had given up birthdays, grunted.

"I'd like to be there." said Elulia.

"Where?"

"In England. It's only for three days," she wheedled.

"But who will clean the toilets?"

"Hervé will before he starts in the morning. And again at night."

"Impossible!"

"I want to go," said Elulia stubbornly. "She may not last another year."

"And you won't last another minute if you go on like this." said J.C. stepping forward.

But, Elulia was not to be browbeaten. "I'm talking to your mother." she said.

"And I'm talking to you," yelled J. C., dancing about."You're fired."

"But, but," said Madam S.

"Get out," shouted J.C. "I'll not have servants talk to me like that."

"Servants?" snapped Elulia.

"Yes, servants."

"I'm not your bloody servant."

"We're busy; we need her," wailed Madam S.

"She should know her place," retorted J.C., "which is in the bloody toilet."

"You," said Elulia, with dignity, "can stick my loo brush right up your arse and scrub your mouth out."

And switching on her walkman to eliminate argument, she strode away to pack.

The DAILY NEWS

Monday 4th August 1992   20p

OLYMPIC MEDALISTS
IN DRUGS FURORE

Allegations that Peter and Sandy, Smart camp's Champion Couriers and gold medal hopes, are on performance enhancing drugs was strongly denied today in a statement from Smartcamp Stadium.

'They are natural born couriers; the statement read. They have all the attributes that make a champion courier, being idle, slovenly, dishonest, shifty, wheedling and downright insolent. They have no need of drugs to increase these virtues.

A spokesman for DATA, the Drug and Additives Testing Authority stated. 'We found Sandy's blood to contain a blend of nicotine and alcohol and tests out at 16° proof showing a preference for fortified wine and gin. Peter's showed a diet high in Mars Bars, potatoes and salad cream and these substances obliterate our tests for anabolic steroids.

UNCLE, the Union and National Couriers League, commented. 'We had hoped for definite results to quell the controversy.
So many young couriers look on Sandy and Peter as their idols and positive tests would have destroyed their worlds. Negative tests would give them faith to continue the struggle against their clients.

What could be the final word on the subject was made by Fred Smart-Camp, owner and MD of the firm. 'Drugs?' he sneered, 'You kidding, boy?' On what we pay our couriers they can't even afford an asprin.

A Courier's Reports are Never...

Sandy was busy packing donated grub into fridge and boxes.

As I posted a notice about the abuse of drugs at the Olympics, I wondered at the gullibility of the public who seemed to believe anything that was published.

Immediately following my invented screed about our distressing circumstances we had clients fighting to give us things.

Some delivered boxes of goodies to our tent. Others left food in their fridges that were not just leftovers but had obviously been purchased for us. Some even asked us subtly what our favourite food was and others left items such as chocolate and wine, that they could easily have carried home.

Or was it done as payment for helping them to enjoy their holiday and my notice indicated that we would not be insulted by a tip.

Perhaps it was in gratitude for relieving them of their kids for a few hours and educating them. In which case we had earned it the hard way.

"Tell us a story." demanded Josephine, as we sat in the kid's tent during a shower.

"We are supposed to be having a quiz." I replied.

"Piss the quiz." interjected Miriam succinctly.

So, to prevent another spate of bad language, I started quickly.

"There was this girl called Red Riding Hood."

"That's kids' stuff." called Jeffrey.

"Yeah, you can stuff that." said Daphne, who had quiet, shy, well-spoken parents. It made me wonder what they were like in private, but I persevered.

"She was taking, to her grandmother, a bag of groceries..."

"I've heard that one," interrupted Valerie.

"...which she had stolen from Tesco's."

They went thoughtful.

"Are you sure?" asked Valerie.

"Yes," I said, "I know because it was Tuesday. On Fridays she robbed Sainsbury's".

They went quiet.

"And as she walked through the woods she met a wolf."

"I know what a wolf is."

"Who said, - you're a pretty girl; what are you doing in a place like this?"

"I know that kind of wolf." put in Muriel, who was fourteen and well developed for her age.

"Visiting grandma" replied Red.

"I'll come with you." said the wolf.

"Like hell you will," retorted Red, "my granny eats cruds like you for breakfast."

"I have Snookie-pops with added vitamins." said Rory, who

understood a word here and there.

"So she went on her way but the wolf took a short cut, got to the cottage first, tied up grandma and bundled her into a cupboard."

They sat around frustratedly seeking something to correct but it was my story.

"and, dressed in a wig and grandma's dressing gown, the wolf let Red in and with a squeaky voice said, 'have you got the loot from Sainsbury's?' 'Tesco's' Red corrected him and asked, 'what's that shivering, stuttering noise in the cupboard. My teeth, replied the disguised wolf, I'm cleaning them in a tub of ice cream."

"I like ice cream," put in Rory.

"Shut up," said Josephine, "what happened then?"

"Let me pour you some whisky, said Red and, moving behind the wolf, she brained him with the bottle, which shows that little girls are not so easily fooled these days. Then she released grandma and they searched his pockets."

"That's stealing." said Jeffrey.

"It's also assault with a dangerous weapon, illegal use of home-made liquor and impeding a cop in the execution of his duty." I said.

"Was he a cop." asked Valerie?

"They found his I.D. showing he was an undercover agent from Sainsbury's".

"What did they do then?" queried Josephine.

"They dropped him down a well and decided not to rob Sainsbury's anymore."

"That's good", said Muriel, who liked a happy ending.

"Is that it?" asked a disappointed Jeffrey.

"No, I said, "they decided to swipe stuff from the Co-op in future as the security was not so hot. Granny was a good fence and needed the money because her pension was insufficient to run her Ferrari."

"What's the moral?" asked Valerie, "these stories always have a moral."

A Courier's Reports are Never...

"The moral is that if you are in the Co-op and see a girl in a red coat, call the nearest cop and tell him that she is a shoplifter."

"We will, we will" chorused the kids.

Which shows that perhaps kids are still easy to fool.

- O -

CHILDRENS COURIERS WEEKLY REPORTS

Site Name: St. Armand   Date: 7th August

Couriers: Sandy and Peter   Numbers: Lots

Venue on Site: Dustbin enclosure

Advertised Programme: Sunday: Painting. Wednesday: Sports Day. Thursday; Campsite quiz.

General summary of week: Sunday: had meeting to decorate ceiling of the tent but it was not very successful as we got tired of holding the kids up in the air. However they were happy and went psychedelically off home.

Wednesday; sports day with Heavenly; we only had six kids against their twelve bigger ones but we did well as we adopted dirty tactics, even though some of their girls must have been on anabolic steroids.

Thursday; told them a fairy story then had a quiz. A Dutch parent, Mr. Groenewald, insisted on leaving his two baffled— looking children who did not speak English, to take part in the quiz. He had previously refrained from bringing them to the sports day as he felt that they would not understand it. He seems to think in Double Dutch.

Any incidents or comments

The minimal sports facilities provided by the site are being used constantly by the animateur for his events; but we go to the adjacent beach which is better.

Have bought hooks, weights and line for catching crabs as the kids are addicted to it. Current record held by five boys is 125 crabs in one hour, and we are thinking of buying torches so that they can do it at night.

- O -

Edith was fooling around with Hervé but he was too pissed for it to register.

Since Elulia's departure he had begun to consume an excessive amount of lunch which, added to the effect of his breakfast brandy, caused him to stagger around in the afternoons as he worked up an appetite to drink his dinner.

We heard her call to him as we waved goodbye to Shipwreck Wicks.

A Courier's Reports are Never...

"Coo-eee, Hervé," she intoned in a sickly way, "I've ironed your shirts".

As we had always seen him wearing the same shirt we looked at her in a baffled manner.

"Well someone has to look after him." she excused herself as she retreated and we went off to scour Wicks' mobile.

"I wonder what they've left us." said Sandy.

"A hairdryer and various bottles and jars," I replied, then as I checked the make-up case, "but I don't think it's for us as they've also left a load of cash."

And I went back for something to pack it in and said goodbye to the Dutch lads.

"We had a terrific time." the eldest said, as he lowered their flag. This was another bra as they ran up a new one every day.

Mrs. Crouch had told me that she enjoyed her holiday because her teenage daughters had made some nice friends and were hardly ever at her tent. I wondered if she had never noticed their fluttering underwear or steadily decreasing lingerie. Or perhaps she felt that their virginity was a small price to pay for peace.

And peace returned to our enclave with the departure of The Unutterably Foul.

"We like this place," he commented, having reduced his tent to a slum and its environs to a rubbish dump in order to feel at home, "we'll be back next year."

And so saying he took a farewell swipe at the barrier and left me with a determination to be elsewhere for the next season.

The DAILY NEWS

Monday 16th August 1992   20p

NEIL KINNOCK FOR SMARTCAMP AT ST.ARMAND

Neil Kinnock some time ago.

It was today leaked from Labour Headquarters that the former leader of the party is looking for alternative employment and is considering working as a courier for Smartcamp at St.Armand.

The idea was placed in his mind at a debate in Parliament during which conservative backbenchers passed him completed Smartcamp application forms with the cries of 'go to hell'

Asked why he considered this job he replied, 'I have worked for the good of the public for long enough and now I would like to make my own fortune by working as a courier for Smartcamp; a response which shows the style of reasoning which has got the Labour Party where it is today.

He enlarged on his decision by stating, 'I intend to live dangerously, boyo. Glynis will kill me if she finds out that I want to get Sandy in labour.'

131

A Courier's Reports are Never...

"Are you hunting Hervé?" I asked.

Edith looked guiltily at the Alsatian she held on a lead.

"No," she said, "this poor dog needs exercise."

It had been shut away for the last month since it had shaken the poodle around screaming like a football supporter's rattle. The poodle, so heavily bandaged that it would have done credit to a mummy's tomb, was receiving much love and attention and Hervé was receiving much loaded vet's bills and therefore locking his dog away from temptation.

I had been writing a notice about Kinnock when Mr.Huggett hopped up and said that the electrics had once again cut out. I told him how to trip them on and promised to find the electrician as the problem was getting too frequent.

Then sighed and displayed my notice which the Alsatian immediately urinated on. I knew it was not a political comment as the dog was French.

"I think Hervé's cleaning the toilets." said Edith.

And there he was, up to his elbows in scouring powder, his face as pale as Harpic and his gills as green as a vegetarians vomit.

"Zees bludding electrics." he said, and we ambled about looking for the source of the trouble.

In a random manner he flicked switches, circuit breakers and fuses like an automation whose mind is nowhere.

"Et mus' be ze bludding junction box." he said. So I followed him to a large cover set in a concrete slab behind tent eleven and helped him lift it.

The stench was dreadful.

"Oh, zere eet is." he exclaimed, pointing at a square object submerged in the filth. Wires led to it and turd's floated above, but he seemed pleased as he hauled it to the surface.

" Zere is perhaps water in eet."

"It's bound to short out in that muck."

"You could be right." he said, dropping it on the side and falling in.

It was fortunate he didn't go head first. Having dropped the box, he straightened suddenly, went dizzy, tangled his feet in the wires and fell across the pit. Then he held the opposite side as his body submerged and his feet touched bottom. Up to his armpits in crap, it was a sight that would have made Dan's day but, whereas the latter would have dropped the cover on him, I merely stepped away from his splashes and addressed

A Courier's Reports are Never...

him.

"I've never known anyone like you for getting in the shit." I said.

It was something I couldn't fail to notice.

- O -

SMARTCAMP HOLIDAYS

Couriers Weekly Report

Site Name: St. Armand   Report N°: 11

Couriers: Peter and Sandy

Week Ending: 7th August

(Summarise your week including details of Weather, Site and Client Problems, Facilities and Competitors)

The eight Dutch teenagers on the next plot have a group of plastic gnomes behind which is a hidden speaker which quacks at passing females. The women they attract look like garden gnomes and walk like ducks and the ensuing daily chat is driving the Heavenly families living opposite bonkers. On the quite untrue pretext of being kept awake all night by carousing young Hollanders, the clients phoned Heavenly Head Office demanding a hotel near Caen and got it. And to reinforce their case they daily complained to the Heavenly couriers who, instead of confronting the Dutch lads, took their complains to the site owners. Beleaguered by hordes of campsite clients, hounded by Heavenly Head Office, couriers and clients, the owners are now at daggers drawn with Heavenly.

In addition, the owners tend to treat their site staff in a high handed manner which led to an altercation with the toilet cleaning lady who took umbrage and handed in her loo brush with an appropriate comment as to where they should place it, and then she took off like a stain threatened with harpic.

As she was living with the site handyman he is now wandering round in an alcoholic

haze, muttering Gaelic curses and baying at the moon. As penance for his sexual excesses with the loolady, he now has to clean the toilets in the early morning.

There is a moral there somewhere but I can't find it.

The only current area of sanity is the fruitcake of a cook who is providing meals at the right price and speaking to no One except his stove with which he has rapport.

As it is high season, the owners use this as an excuse to flash about in a panicky uncoordinated way, sweat profusely, and be abrupt, with all and sundry. To counter this we solve our own problems, nod to them affably as they dash past and ignore their looks

133

which say that we can't be working properly as we are not frantic.

On Wednesday the Dutch teenagers left amidst much wailing and quacking of females; and gnashing by Heavenly clients who must now invent some other excuse to obtain rebates.

The Unutterably Foul also left in a triple roar of exhaust, a scream of engines and a terrifying, "see you next year."

Our clients" competition for lost property is being led by Shipwreck Wicks whose wife left hairdryer, conditioner, spray and make up case but we feel that the £125 cash was taking an unfair advantage.

Our prize comment of the week was made in a phone call to the site office when Mr. Porridge asked that the wardrobe full of food and clothes be handed to the Unutterably Foul with whom he had, unbelievably, made friends. "Tell him to post them to me when he gets to England." Porridge said, "he can reclaim the postage from Smartcamp."

Belated comments from relieved clients show that Unutterably was worse than we thought and his statement that teenagers made noise in Dutch in the toilet block at 7 a.m. was pure smokescreen and, if it happened, due to them retaliating. But most of our clients are almost human and enjoyable.

The weather has varied, from days of blistering heat to the odd shower, and clients have reacted accordingly, sometimes being brick red and sometimes dripping wet. It's nice to see them participate.

CHAPTER 17

I couldn't fail to notice her as she stood in the doorway, bulk dimming the light that filtered into reception, face dark with unexpressed anger. Glowering, she had the sort of features that switches out the sun and cast, gloom and despondency like shrouds over all and sundry. But her aura was wasted as it was already raining.

"You're not going to cancel the meeting, are you?" she growled. I listened to rain slamming against the tent, saw canvas shudder as the wind beat, looked at her two little girls with water dripping from their sodden clothes.

"Beach Party." I said, echoing our advertised treat, "with crisps and bottles of pop. Should be fun."

She made that rumbling noise in her throat again. "Just as long as you're not going to cancel."

"Of course not." I soothed her, as one would a wild beast.

And leaving her cubs to whatever pneumonia ridden fate we might devise, she

A Courier's Reports are Never...

shambled off.

It was people like Mrs. Malpas who defeated our system.

What, I asked myself, was the point in my going all the way down to the port to get the local long range forecast so as to advertise club activities that couldn't take place, if unfeeling parents deposited the brats with us as though we were a junior euthanasia clinic. Wild animals took more care of their young that did these domesticated ones who dumped offspring then galloped back to their sties for a bit of breeding space.

It was the same the following Tuesday.

The kids were crazy about crabbing, much to our disgust as, before it was discovered, we took them to the beach where they grovelled in the sand for cockles which Sandy and I subsequently ate. Kids club thereby provided us with a change of diet from clients' leftovers and we had found many ways to cook them.

Cockles are delicious lightly fried with an equal amount of bacon or may be coated in seasoned flour and crisped in shallow heated oil. But the crabs now being caught were too small to provide meat, no matter for how long they were boiled. So we always let them go. But catching them at least occupied the kids without our having to do much apart from thread the hooks and untangle lines woven between neighbouring crab catchers.

So on Tuesday, when the weather was to be scattered gales leading to high seas and lashing breakers, parents brought us nine customers of tender ages, replete with nylon lines sporting vicious hooks, and encouraged us to take them to the shore to balance them on narrow breakwaters and have them crouch over the heaving water to dangle barnacles at seasick crabs.

"You'd think they'd be more concerned." I yelled to Sandy as a six year old, caught by a violent gust, teetered towards a watery death and I leapt to steady her.

"They're thoughtless bastards." replied Sandy, inadvertently repeating Winston's opinion as she dug a hook out of a small boys thumb.

"Thoughtless bastards," Winston had said, "they don't even like you to sleep".

A Heavenly savage had left that morning before the barrier was raised. With his car stuck in the campsite and his distant ferry getting up steam, he was desperate to be away and emoting angry frustration tempered by a desire not to rouse the whole campsite.

He was jumping up and down and tapping on Winston's door each time he landed when he noticed me watching with interest.

"Have you got a key to the barrier?" he asked, pausing in his morning calisthenics for a moment.

A Courier's Reports are Never...

"Yes," I replied, having been slipped one by J.C. in gratitude for not disturbing him with problems every hour on the hour.

So I let the Heavenly victim out and relocked the barrier, but even so he was not content.

"The idle swine," he muttered, "never does anything".

Being in a position to see both sides of the picture, I tried to smooth his feathers.

"Probably stayed up late to welcome a client." I explained.

He snorted in a disbelieving way. "He didn't for me" he said, "I found a note on his door with a plan and a key to my mobile".

He thought back, "I think it was a plan of Normandy."

And so saying, steaming worse than his ferry, he strode to Winston's mobile, picked up the metal gas trolley, repeatedly slammed it beneath the bedroom window and screamed as follows:

"It's alright, you idle swine, don't wake up. I've opened the barrier without you."

Then he violently revved his car and roared off. It is strange what gives some people pleasure.

"Really," said Winston, when I told him later, "I never heard a thing."

I looked at the dents in the mobile and the broken window, recalled the shouts from aroused campers and let him fool me.

"Pity you didn't wake" I said, "he was quite emotional. Probably wanted to give you something."

And also emotional and donatative was Dan.

- O -

CHILDRENS COURIERS WEEKLY REPORT

Site Name: St. Armand   Date: 14th August

Couriers: Sandy and Peter   Numbers: Less as we mislaid a few.

Venue on Site: Local Brothel

Advertised Programme: Saturday; Beach Hunt. Tuesday: another beach Hunt. Thursday; String Hunt. Friday: Boules Tournament.

General Summary of Week: Saturday; in spite of rain

Mrs. Malpas dropped off her two girls for the beach hunt which we had to cancel. We began by using play doe until other kids appeared as the rain stopped, when we had the usual ruckus. Tuesday; Rain, gales, hail and sudden squall but uncaring parents brought nine suffering kids for a hunt on the beach. In a burst of sunshine and only force six wind, we caught crabs and spray but the kids were happy although soggy.

On Thursday we had an aperitif party and sent half the kids off to hide string for the other half, and the other half to hide string for the first half, then sent the second half to look for the first half's string, and the first half to look for the second half's string, which sounds confusing and was as we were all drinking Kir Royale.

On Friday morning our group of mainly up to ten year olds had a boules tournament with plastic boules being hurled hither and thither to the chagrin of French players who were trying to have a serious competition with metal boules, which shows that boules players have no sense of humour. But the kids" parents loved it and took many photos and, with the adults of the species being present, the boules players refrained from acrimonious action.

Any incidents or comments

Little Jeanie Crampton hit a French boules player in the boules with her boule. The hospital has not informed us as to his condition but his wife is threatening legal action. Does the damage waiver cover accidental castration?

- O -

Dan arrived during the afternoon, drew up outside Edith's and saw her snuggling up to Hervé on one of his firm's settees.

Having had enough of Hervé utilising his possessions he popped from his van like a cork from a dipsomaniac's champagne and hurled himself at the door.

Which Hervé had prudently locked.

So as Dan kicked in the door, Hervé threw Edith's potted fern through the back window and followed.

"I love her" said Dan sadly, as he repaired the demonstrations of affection he had inflicted on the mobile, "I even drove her to the ferry."

"Will she come back to you?" Sandy asked.

Dan meditatively struck his thumb with a hammer. "She might," he muttered indistinctly," or she might go back to that frigging frog"

He wrapped his thumb in soiled rag, "that is if he is still alive."

"Do you think there's much chance?" I inquired.

"Not if I get my hands on him."

"No. I mean, of her coming back to you."

A Courier's Reports are Never...

"Not sure," he ruminated, "I don't know why she left. We had a good life together.

"Were you," asked Sandy, looking at his large muscular body, "er, sensitive and gentle with her?"

Dan nodded mournfully, "Kindness itself. Bent to her every whim. Puffins." he added.

"Pardon?"

"Puffins." he repeated and sighed.

Sandy and I looked at each other wondering how to stop him rambling. He was obviously relapsing into delirium. I decided to humour him.

"Nice things puffins." I probed.

"She was crazy about puffins." he explained. "To please her I used to dress up in a puffin costume."

"Demonstrating sensitivity." I said.

"Oh yes. I used to perch on the kitchen table and she would knock me off with a stick".

"I thought she liked puffins?"

"She did. She liked them roasted."

"And you were too big to go in the oven."

He looked at me strangely.

"What a peculiar mind you have." he said.

- O -

Mr. Fosil's mind would have been peculiar had he had one.

He drove all the way from Boulogne in a small open two seater sports car towing a trailer, and arrived with his wife and two children, wind battered and punchy, just before 1 a.m.

"Is the bar open?" he cried, reeling out on cramped legs. His wife and two children painfully followed.

So they limped round to the bar where he cried: "Are you still open?"

"Yes." said the barman

"What would you like. Winklepuss," he asked his wife, who was short and trim with long dark, wind- blown hair.

"Something cool but warming." She deliberated for a while, "a whisk and soda. No, tonic instead. Or rather, with lemonade.

"Right," he said, "and you two?"

"Can I have a beer, Dad?"

"No. Have lemonade."

"And a coke for me."

"Make mine a coke as well, Dad."

"Make mine a rum and coke." said Winklpuss.

"Come on, make up your minds. I'll have a beer. Right," he turned to the barman as the clock chimed. "We would like..". he cried.

"Sorry, we're closed." said the barman.

"But you're not."

"We close at one. Site rules."

"But…."

"Closed." said the barman firmly.

"Look here," said Fosil furiously, "I'm a reporter. I'll write about you in my paper."

"Would you like a photo to go with it?" inquired the barman.

- O -

Clients were still arriving during the early hours from their revised ports as the ferry was not yet repaired.

Thompson and Skinner turned up for adjacent mobiles at 2 a.m., Jackson and Kargo for adjacent tents at 1.30. Which was fortunate, for if I had taken the initial brunt of looking at Jackson during daylight I would have cancelled the next aperitif party rather than expose it to his pernicious influence.

It was bad enough that the malevolent Mrs. Malpas had bought tickets but Kargo bought for the two parties and Jackson was just a brooding presence in a car when Sandy showed them their tent.

A more chirpy presence was Graves.

"What ho," he chirruped, "you must Peter."

"Fame at last." I said.

"The Reverend Bristow told me about you" he burbled, "which is why I'm here with Smartcamp."

A Courier's Reports are Never...

"I thought you said he told you about me"

"Yes. Said to read your notices."

So I showed him today's which was about the pope and he went away cheered as he was C of E.   Also Clown of Europe was Mr. Foyer.

The DAILY NEWS

Monday 18th August 1992   20p

POPE – LATEST

The pope leaving Smartcamp last month.

A report that the Pope is in hospital to give birth to an immaculately conceived child was denied today by a Vatican official.

'The Pope is a normal man just like you and I; he stated, 'and is in hospital for the removal of an ovarian cyst.'

A Courier's Reports are Never...

Sandy waited up until 2.30 a.m., and then collapsed into bed.

"Foyer has probably taken a hotel for the night." she said.

"At last a sensible one" I said, reverting back to blessed sleep. But it was not to be.

"Hammer, hammer, bang, bang, hoy where are you?" went my dream and carried on when I woke.

"Wassat." muttered Sandy, rousing partly.

"Hello, hello, bang, bang, hoy." it went again.

And there on the step was this tubby chap with a bristling moustache and a matching nature.

"Where the hell were you," he demanded, "They said you'd be here to meet me."

"I am here," I said, "and absolutely delighted to meet you?"

"Oh, ah, well then. Show us to our tent, we're tired?"

"May I get dressed or should I come naked?"

He hung about while I grabbed clothes and when sartorially elegant in Smartcamp gauds, I joined him.

"I thought you'd be waiting up." he commented.

"Sandy sat up until 2.30 for you," I said.

"Then why did she stop?"

"Because the police took over. We notified their missing persons' bureau and they are searching the highways."

"Oh dear," he said, "we stopped for a meal."

"They're checking restaurants, cafés, brothels, and all-night cinemas. Tell me; did you come via Fouesnant?"

"No, why?"

"Road blocks," I said, "they would have got you there."

"Oh, dear. I'm sorry to have caused so much trouble."

"No trouble whatsoever," I replied, as I tossed him into his tent in mid-enclave. "I'll just go and call off the manhunt."

- O -

I tried to foist Jackson off onto Edith when I discovered him glaring stonily about outside our reception.

"He's a very rich man." I said.

She pensively rubbed her cheek then scratched her nose, leaving a red smear of blusher.

"Really?" He looks a bit miserable, she said doubtfully.

"They all are. They worry about money."

"Hello," she gave it a try, "I'm Edith."

He turned his unresponsive stare on her.

"Er, ah." she quailed.

"Rich." I murmured.

She leaned in close. "I'd like you on my mailing list."

"Understandable." he replied, turning away.

"Oy, you," his son addressed me from behind the Kids Club board, "what's a beach hunt?"

"We bury the kid with the biggest ears," I said, noting that his head looked like a football trophy, "then we try to find him before the tide comes in."

He never came to Kids Club but the whole family came to the a aperitif party where they stood around like statues in a park and smokers struck matches on them.

But we were too busy and tired to notice.

- O -

The aperitif was a great success.

Somewhat knackered from late nights, early mornings, shopping, preparing, cooking and general client cosseting, we loaded the camper with goodies, drove it to a space by Mr. Foyer's tent, collected all the nearby tables and discharged our consumables onto them.

At 6.30 on the dot, Mr. Huggett, hopped up at our front, followed closely by most of the others and festivities began.

They whooped and hollered, squealed when a champagne cork popped and encouraged me to blast them even higher.

"Get one over that tree." chirped Graves.

Instead I landed a high one on Fosil as he drove in fast and late and he squawked and swerved into Huggett's tent.

But Huggett only laughed and they pulled Fosil out and held a hotdog sausage against his eye. "Just as good as steak." chortled Graves, and Jackson stared stonily on.

And so the evening pressed on with cheap champagne disguised with a dash of blackcurrant juice oiling their throats and helping them laugh. The kids, stuffed with hotdogs, got out from under our feet and went on a string hunt, all except Jug eared Jackson who worried about being buried.

The time went quickly in drunken revelry. Mrs. Malpas glowered as Thompson and Skinner used her barbecue in an abortive attempt at cooking. Everyone cheered their charred efforts and the sound built up until we became aware of the competition.

Jean-Claud, noticing that our party had exceeded the statutory eight p.m., sent Springheel Jaques in the loudspeaker wagon to broadcast his evening's treat and thereby seduce our clients. As it rumbled incoherently towards us, his broadcast was taken as a personal slight by the next door animateur who ran to his van, engaged full volume, and caught up with Springheel on the other side of the fence, just as he reached our tents.

Unable to hear themselves laugh, the Smart campers stood in mute amazement, as the two vehicles turned to face each other like knight's chargers and shook and trembled with the volume as the rival animateurs screamed profanities at each other. Our clients watched motionless, all except, Mrs. Jackson who placed a large flat foot in Edith's back as the latter leaned against her husband and, with a quick thrust, kicked her over the Malpas' barbecue.

It was the cue they all needed. Babble resumed as they picked hot coal off Edith and shouted encouragement to Springheel.

"Come," I said, handing Sandy into the camper, "let's leave before it gets out of control."

We drove off for a quiet nightcap with Winston and Minnie before dropping into bed and blameless slumber.

And dreams of jousting Knights, banquets and roasting peasants. Of such things are notices made.

Court Circular

Smartcamp Reception   *14ᵗʰ August 1992*

Crown Prince Peter, pretender to the House of Smartcamp, was in residence for one hour after the formal 9am opening, to attend to matters of state including issue of treasure chest items, compilation of reports and receiving of deputations from loyal subjects.
In attendance was Edith de Mucus, lady in waiting.

Victualing Tour: Her Serene Highness, Princess Sandy, after rising and visiting the royal chamber, joined the Prince in a tour of the Hypermarket at Corentin to obtain victuals for the Royal Banquet. They were attended by the store security officer and their departure was aided by two gendarmes.

Royal Banquet: The evening commenced with the arrival of the Prince and Princess in the state coach after which they dispensed to attendant courtiers largess and champagne amid the ceremony of the High Corks. The opening was enhanced by the arrival of Chief-Scribe Fosil in his Landau, who parked on the drawbridge of the Manoir de Hugget amid much bustle and hilarity.
In attendance were Count Kargo, Lord Jackson and Professor Friar Malpas.

At the ceremony of Crisps and Nuts the following were received: Squire Graves representing the Divine Court of St. Bristow, Dominec Groanewald representing the Very Low Countries, and Father Murphy of Ballyguinnes representing a human being.

Victuals dispensed to the grovelling hordes included smoked dogfish, flavoured cat-meat, steamed hedgehog bait and stewed offal on toast. The children ate breaded giblets then embarked on a hunt for string which was used to hang the smallest.

The Duke of Skinner, Earl Thompson and entourage, then closed the proceedings with an offering of charred sausage bits and all collapsed in drunken jesting.

The Royal Party then retired to Smartcamp Apartments to take hot cocoa and aspirins for the right royal headaches. Minnie Heavenly, Mistress of the Royal Bedchamber, was in attendance.

A Courier's Reports are Never...

<u>SMARTCAMP HOLIDAYS</u>

Couriers Weekly Report

Site Name: St. Armand   Report N° 12

Couriers: Peter and Sandy

Week Ending: 14th August

(Summarise your week including details of Weather, Site and Client Problems, Facilities and Competitors)

For a supposedly quiet site this place is unbelievably raucous and the decibel level must, contravene the E E C rate for noise pollution. During the day the animateur travels through the site with a loudspeaker van, alternating his shouted announcements with blasts of melody; and in the evening his loudspeaker bellows instructions at imbecile campers embroiled in bingo, lotto, or just sitting stupefied. When they are let out at 1 a.m., they surge back through the camp releasing their pent up volubility to the irritation of dormant campers. The French love it but our clients complain and the owners keep the racket going until 1 a.m. as it helps the bar takings.

Our Mr. Fosil staggered into the bar at one minute past, having just arrived but they refused him a beer. "I've just driven from Boulogne." he told them. "We're still closed," said the barman. So much for Anglo-French relations.

Jean-Claud, alias J.C., also known as Jesus Christ Superstar, is nice and friendly to us but less than 100% to the staff. The handyman, who knows the vagaries and foibles of the drains and electrics, muttered with many oaths and much throat clearing, that he will not be here next year. The owners are struggling now but next season should see them really suffer. Clients' competition for the most forgotten luggage is dying down. Mr. Leaf left his wife's stockings under the bed but fortunately she was not wearing them, and Mr. Wenche's forgotten shoes were the wrong size for me.

Our present, scourge is Mrs. Malpas who has a round fat head set on a round fat body and looks like a cottage loaf with two dead currants for eyes. She brought her two little girls to Children's' Club, during a sudden storm, for an advertised Beach Party and stood with arms folded and an expression daring us to cancel the meeting. Perhaps the children are heavily insured.

Another favourite is Mr. Jackson who wanted to be, and is, in the next tent, to Mr. Kargo. Mr. Jackson looks like a particularly malignant stone statue and varies his expression by glaring in different directions so that one has, at times, a different profile view; best not to stand in front as receiving the full brunt is conducive to sleepless nights. And so he stands and glowers, with dog stains on his trouser leg, while his wife, an ungainly lumbering creature, lurches at his side and tries not to step on their very unprepossessing son who is equally humourless, and will most likely finish up as a hangman.

I only wish that this bunch had been here during the Unutterably Foul era as they would have quelled him just by being there.

Mr. Kargo was a nice chap and very apologetic, probably because of his neighbours, who must have been relatives as no one has friends like that. But when Mr. Jackson went he left a remarkably clean tent which leads me to think that they slept standing up in the corner.

I put Dr. Bath into tent number eleven, as doctors are notoriously lax in hygiene and also are used to perusing peoples' private parts, and he was perfectly happy and pitched gaily on and off the windsurfer whenever the tide was in, possibly in an attempt to dislodge germs.

Our clients' latest competition is to see who can arrive the latest. Times of 1 and 2 a.m. became commonplace until the advent of Mr. Foyer. He hammered on our door at 3 a.m. demanding his tent. "Stopped off to shop and have a meal." he explained winsomely. Fortunately J. C. had given me a barrier key so he drove in and was able to create the maximum disturbance. We got up at 7 a.m., worked and shopped for the aperitif party, and in the afternoon, while making sandwiches, Mrs. Foyer came for her money back. "My husband's too tired to be there." she said. We never saw him again, even though we held the party outside his tent with much whooping and banging of champagne corks; and then Sandy and I collapsed into a dreamless coma.

Mr. Rossiter, an imaginative man with a nice family, has found a new use for the Children's Club bags. They are exactly the right size for carrying 2 milk bottles from the shop. Put that in the brochure; it is good advertising.

CHAPTER 18

The weather became foul and our clients adjusted their attitudes to match.

Existing clients would ask what we had done with the sun and new arrivals would tell us how much better the weather was in England; accusingly as though, to their detriment, we had sold the local sunshine.

Winston, of course, asked his gripers why they hadn't brought good weather with them. "Left it in England, did you? How bloody stupid." he would snarl, getting in first. I enjoyed his repartee, for which he had a natural feel and his timing was good.

"Your map's wrong." shouted a client, arriving fractious, late and in a downpour.

"I haven't got a map." replied Winston.

"You have," said the arrival, taken aback, "the one in your brochure."

A Courier's Reports are Never...

"I haven't got a brochure."

"You have," said the baffled arrival, "the Heavenly brochure."

"Oh, the Heavenly brochure," replied Winston, looking enlightened, "why didn't you say so?"

His clients at least knew immediately where they stood. On soggy, slippery quicksand.

Our clients stood on a soaking campsite with a quagmire, courtesy of the Unutterably Foul, like a muddy moat in front of their tents, with solid sheets of rain beating at them and became highly vocal.

"Where's the gymnasium you advertised?"

"We're paying a lot of money for this weather."

"That Jacuzzi doesn't work."

"The sauna's broken."

"The bar's too small."

"Our tent's not in the sun." said Mr. White from tent five, which was beneath low trees and never dried out.

"What sun?" I asked.

"Well, if it was sunny, it wouldn't be in it." he replied, which illustrates how they sit and think up problems when the weather's bad.

So we told them of indoor swimming pools, indoor golf links, indoor shopping centres and indoor bowling alleys.

Which had the advantage that they took the kids off for the day and kids club meetings became distant heinous memories.

- O -

CHILDRENS COURIERS WEEKLY REPORT

Site Name: St. Armand   Date: 21st August

Couriers: Sandy and Peter   Numbers: None

Venue on Site: Absinthe Den

Advertised Programme: Monday: Stock Car Racing. Wednesday; High Wire Walking. Friday; Deep Sea Diving.

General summary of week:

No kids turned up, probably due to the weather.

A Courier's Reports are Never...

- O -

And with the absence of children, I was able to utilise their tent for my early morning exercise sessions and watch Hervé creep furtively away from the consoling embrace of Edith's mobile.

"The two-timing swine," said Sandy, who was corresponding with Elulia and knew that she would return in the winter, "and Edith is twenty years older than him."

"But he's catching up fast." I said, having been able to discern the lines of wear, tear and fatigue even in the weak wet light of the dawn. "She's beginning to look younger than him."

"Probably having injections." said Sandy ambiguously, and we left it at that.

But Edith no longer crept round and fraternised with her clients. Her cries of 'pay is late' or 'only crusts to eat', were no longer heard as she fed off Hervé. Clients could stroll past her mobile without being entangled in a web, or having a net drop on them, and the sight of Edith crawling to the showers of a morning was not pretty.

"Rain?" she said to me, being too preoccupied to notice, "what rain?"

"I've had enough of rain," snapped Mrs. Eals, "we want a transfer to the sun."

"It's raining everywhere." I said regretfully. Regretfully because I would have loved to be rid of her.

She 'tsk, tsked', and thrust a newspaper under my nose. "It's not raining there." she said.

It was open to show a picture of the Duchess of York reclining on a Sunny beach with an American friend sucking her big toe.

"That's the Bahamas or Philippines or some such where," I said. "I'll try to get you there but I can't guarantee a toe job." But without deigning to reply she strode off, packed and disappeared when we weren't looking.

And we drew a veil over the rest of the rotten week and disappeared into the following one.

The DAILY NEWS

Monday 28th August 1992   20p

DENIAL

Indignation was today expressed by Smartcamp Palace at the publication by several leading newspapers of pictures showing Sandy topless on a beach with an American sucking her big toe.

'This kind of exposure attracts the wrong sort of client who then expects to much of our couriers; said Fred Smart-Camp, the firm's owner, 'besides which if there is any sucking to be done around here, I'll do it.'

President Bush is understood to be concerned by the development.
'This sucking slob is obviously going to use his familiarity with Sandy as a ploy to enter the Presidential race; he stated.
'We do not need another candidate, especially one who shows such an intimate knowledge of foreign affairs,'

His sentiments were echoed by Governor Clinton. 'What's this guy after?' he demanded of a hall packed with delegates, 'is he trying to outdo my record?'

Another type of sucker.

Meanwhile Peter has remained unruffled by the controversy.

'Sandy has given me a full and convincing explanation of the whole unfortunate incident; he said.

'She was crawling along this beach searching for the bra she had lost during Children's Club when a short-sighted American mistook her raspberry flavoured nail polish for his lost ice lolly.

It's all quite simple really.'

A Courier's Reports are Never...

Site: St. Armand   Date: 21st August

Couriers: Peter and Sandy

Clients Name: Eals

(Detail the complaint / Problem and action taken)

Mrs. Eals had a bad case of acne as a child which pitted both her face and her nature. She resembles a baked albino walnut, being as hard on the centre as on the outside, and controls her handsome but boyish husband by sudden shifts of mood and temperament. Her two young sons, due to inheriting a tractable nature from Dad and exposure to mother's fickle whims, are pleasant, colourless, characterless objects lacking in initiative or leadership. The matriarch's rules are law.

Ensconced in number 7, our best mobile, she fretted about the weather and muttered about clearing off to find the sun. I spoke to her on the pool terrace one evening. "We might clear off," she said, "find some sun and stay at hotels and things. We've seen everything around here within a ten mile radius." "I like the port," commented her husband, flicking ash from his cheap cigar into the pool, "full of yachts and things."

"We have a lot of camps in the Vendee," I told her, "you could perhaps transfer." "Maybe," she replied, "but I fancy a hotel or two." "We'll come here in our own yacht one day," enthused Mr. Eals, as he tossed his cigar butt at a passing swimmer, "I'm saving up for one."

Next morning they were gone. Taking the mobile key with them, they walked out leaving a filthy mobile in a state of chaos. But she had said that if they left and found no sun they would be back, so we left the hovel awaiting their return as the long-range forecast was for rain, storms and anti-Eals weather.

Two days later we went to buy local corkscrews as the ones supplied by stores were snapping like clients on an inclement day. On the way back into camp we collected a newly arrived fax that said that Mrs. Eals had cancelled her holiday with us. It seems that she had obtained bookings of 2 or 3 days at various Vendee sites to enable her to view everything within a camp's ten mile radius, and then move on thus allowing couriers to do her housework.

At our reception an irate Mr. and Mrs. Jails awaited us. Pacing out into the rain at intervals to improve his soaked appearance, he shouted, "where the hell were you?" "We've been waiting hours." yelled his spouse, not to be outdone. It seems that they were sudden impulsive transferees from Carnac who had arrived before we were notified. I put them in the camp bar, paid £5 for a round of coffee, and we galloped off to the Eal's tip to make it habitable. I also phoned Head office who admitted to having transferred the Jails but, to the date of their leaving this site, we have not received a fax

A Courier's Reports are Never...

telling us that they would be inflicted.

We rapidly converted the mobile to our usual immaculate standard, escorted the Jails there and pointed out the view, the amenities, the closeness of attractive towns, and lit the gas fire to dry out the family and improve their son's asthma. Then retired with obsequious solicitude.

Over the next week we plied them with Our Winsome Ways and generally cultivated them. I actually liked them and found them, once dry, delightful.

They, in turn, responded. They want to book next year's holiday as soon as they receive a new brochure, and thereby take advantage of the special book-in-October offer. I have suggested Sarlat as being suitable for persons of their undoubted excellent taste. So do send them an early brochure, perhaps with a personal note. As for Mrs. Eals; send her a brochure for Euroslops. They deserve each other.

Footnote: If you ever see a yacht that looks like a floating rubbish dump, shout "Hello Mr.Eals."

- O -

SMARTCAMP HOLIDAYS

Couriers Weekly Report

Site Name:	St.Armand

Report N°: 13

Couriers: Peter and Sandy

Week Ending: 21st August

(Summarise your week including details of Weather, Site and Client Problems, Facilities and Competition)

Our clients complain about the lack of facilities. The Jacuzzi never worked, the pool is small and overcrowded, the bar and terrace have been taken over by the animateur and the French to the exclusion of our lot, the gymnasium was never very much but now the equipment has been pushed into a corner so that the animatuer can lead his rabble in bingo, lotto or cards. When the bar is available it is packed with teenagers and loud music so that there is no place for adults to have a quiet drink. I think we can expect a few complaints, particularly as the weather has been changeable for the last two weeks.

The French are pulling out fast, as their holiday draws to a close. And now the campsite decides that it wants the English. Suddenly announcements are in English and I was asked to tell our people of a coach trip to the indoor swimming pool. They had hired a 50 seater and found not enough aquatic frogs to fill it. And they, in their loudspeaker van, shouted in English that a disco would be held one evening. We were

A Courier's Reports are Never...

fraternising with clients due to depart the following day, when their disgruntled kids returned to say that the disco was cancelled. Next day, I asked why. The owner had some obscure explanation that the adjacent site was holding one, so ours had to be cancelled. But no reason was given to the disappointed kids. These people don't seem to have an act to get together.

Mrs. Suds came and told us miracle couriers that they have a lot of wasps around their tent, then waited for us to snap our fingers and exorcise them. Her husband had a puncture. He said, "It might be a valve, or a cut, or maybe a nail or something but would you phone a garage and get a firm price to repair it?"

And constantly the blame for this inclement weather besmirches our doorstep.

On Tuesday we expected six displaced Roscoff people, but Head Office was unable to tell us which way they were rerouted. 3 lots arrived at 3.30 p.m. as we finished lunch, so we stayed open for the rest. And open, and open, until at 9.30 we had to visit next day's departures. At 10.15 two more lots arrived and complained because we were not at reception to greet them. So we stayed open until, driven by exhaustion, we fell asleep at 2.30 a.m. Our next arrival appeared at 10.30 a.m. as we were cleaning mobiles and acted surprised. "Surely you knew we were on an overnight ferry, after all, you rerouted us." What is it? Is the computer fighting back? On Wednesday, having learnt, we went to bed at midnight, and left a note for our outstanding arrivals to call us. They turned up on Thursday at 3.30 p.m. "You expected us yesterday?" they said, "but your office organised a stopover at Dole. And a funny thing; they didn't know we were coming." The computer is definitely fighting back. Or is it on holiday.

Mr. Crunch and entourage arrived in two cars, four adults and four large teenagers; they filled the mobile and jammed the cars against the side; then sat and listened to a raging thunderstorm as they rocked about. Next day Mr. Crunch accosted me. "Do you have a mobile further up the slope, out of the trees?" he asked. "My wife's claustrophobic." With that mob herded in, I think I would be; but I didn't tell him. Instead I said, "feel lucky, the people in the bottom mobiles have to wear life jackets at high tide." He's only here for three nights but is considering requesting a transfer. I think that our clients are beginning to fight back as well.

Tremendous storm on wednesday night. Sounds of thunder, lightning and screaming clients. On thursday they muttered at us but didn't mutiny, even though it rained all day. Friday was sunny end soothed them slightly but there is still talk of transferring to the sun; even though we assured them that the storms are throughout France. Mrs.Eals has the most strident voice and a battered husband. You will hear more of her if you care to read the special report.

Campsite is less crowded with phased closure of the French holidays. Our clients watch them go with suspicion; they seem to think they are off to a secret source of sun. One can't trust these foreigners.

CHAPTER 19

Having dashed into the next week, we wished we hadn't.

We were inundated with wind, rain, gales and complaints much as during the week from which we had escaped. But this one was rendered more vile by the French campers pulling out and allowing Jean-Claud to see the devastation they had wrought to his future inheritance. And this shortened his fuse close to explosive level.

At first we weren't aware of this as we got him to rearrange the gym so that equipment could be used. The animateur was no longer monopolising the room due to withdrawing his services suddenly. The previous week he had objected to his rival animateur holding a disco on the same evening and had gone next door to sort the matter out. But his rival had sorted him out in much the same way as the Alsatian had sorted out his poodle and he had retired early to convalesce and repair his broken leg.

It was nice to hear that they had settled their dispute about who was the better, and the site was remarkably quiet now that Springheel's electronic mouth was withdrawn.

But the lack of noise was equated, in J.C.s mind, with a drop in income and he became as morose and jumpy as a client on a wet and windy day.

Of both of these, we had surfeits.

They trooped steadily to reception to ask if we had space on a site in the sun and receive our latest suggestions as to where to find indoor pursuits. I re-advertised similar children's club activities as before, as this proved to be a winning formula and attracted no one. And listened gravely as clients bitched and fabricated in attempts to get on our special reports.

- O -

CHILDRENS COURIERS WEEKLY REPORT

Site Name: St. Armand   Date: 28th August

Couriers: Sandy and Peter   Numbers: not anyone

Venue on Site: First aid isolation hut.

Advertised Programme: Monday; Erotic Hunt. Wednesday: Intimate Party. Friday; Carnal Games. NOTE: Due to outbreaks of foreign lurgie, all children must be in possession of valid rabies certificates and have had leprosy vaccinations.

General Summary of Week

Strange but there seems to be a marked lack of interest in the club and one wonders if it is worth continuing.

- O -

SPECIAL REPORT

Site: St.Armand   Date: 28th August

Couriers: Peter and Sandy

Clients Name: Mr. Gobbi and Mr. Clog

(Detail the complaint/problem and action taken)

"It's that vicious site dog," said Mr. Gobbi, referring to the amiable hearthrug that the kids ride around the bar, "it bit our child. It's the last straw. The first straw was a pong from the bogs, the second straw was that this site is not Benemaas and does not have squeakers and kiss-me-quick hats in the Treasure Chest, and the third straw was the weather.

"Why should we pay the same price for this place as we would for Benemaas?" said his twitching, nervous wife, speaking of the site five miles away. "I'm sure they have better weather." I phoned Michael who transferred them to the Vendee. "Tell him to send me an account." said Mr. Gobbi, obviously not intending to pay when I informed him of the extra cost clients had to pay to cover overheads. I handed him over to Michael who explained, no cash no transfer. "You've got me over a barrel, what's your name," snarled Mr. Gobbi, not knowing he could find it on the notepaper under the title, Managing Director, "you'll hear more of this; I'll have you fired." He was much braver over the phone. "I've nothing against you, you understand," he told me, "I suppose you like it here." I gave him my opinion that it was the best site I had been on and that finished our affinity.

Mr. Clog heard that his crony in the next tent had managed a transfer so we phoned Michael who arranged one for him. "I really wanted to be in Benemaas," he moaned, "tried there originally but they had no places." He never took up his booking in the Vendee as, next morning, he visited Benemaas and fixed himself up for a week with Tentin Holidays.

Action taken: I asked to see the child's bite but Mr. Gobbi said that there was no point as the skin wasn't broken. Phoned Head Office for the transferees and was non-committal about how this site compares with Benemaas and about our charges, except to say that this site appeals to me. Wished them both a happy holiday.

Mr. Gobbi muttered that he would write a complaint but doubted that he would get his money back. Stated that he was a journalist and had ways of extracting revenge.

I asked the site owner to investigate the complaints about, the sewage smell but forgot to ask him to alter the weather.

Had a word with the site dog who denied the whole incident and refused my request to bite Mr. Gobbi as it is not vicious.

But some clients were adaptable, put up rows of tables and umbrellas in the Unutterably Swamp, and sat in hats and rain-coats barbecuing meat on coals that sizzled with drizzle; and then sang songs much as Gene Kelly does on inclement days.

One has to admire British fortitude and impervious skin.

The DAILY NEWS

Monday 2nd September 1992   20p

WEATHER

The cause of the high winds at present sweeping the world was outlined today at an emergency meeting of WOW (World Organisation for Weather) when blame was laid squarely on Britain's doorstop.

'The winds are due; said Professor I. Bulluw-Knott, president of the Geographic National Union (GNU), 'to holes in the ozone layer allowing pressure to escape and certain areas of air to rise.
This causes high velocity air to rush in to take its place giving us high winds and unsettled weather.'

He went on to explain in detail the reasons for the holes in the ozone. 'It is due; he stated, 'to the very strong deodorant sprays and disinfectants that are used to clean and fumigate Mucus mobiles because of the type of clients they accept.

Normal cleaners have no effect on the foul detritus these people use to clog up the vans and Edith has no alternative but to use these destructive types of cleaning material.

Typical northen French weather.

A demand by the delegates to have these mobiles banned was overruled by the Chairman.

'A few of the Mucus clients are quite nice; he said. 'Why should they suffer because of the majority?'

A Courier's Reports are Never...

To explain why the weather was so spiteful I published a notice, then went to phone for a transfer for our latest belly-aches. And, on my way to the phone, heard J.C. warming up his guns with a broadside at Dan.

"I'm going to ban you from the site." he shouted.

J.C. had at last begun to notice that Hervé was acting in a peculiar manner. Hervé never walked along roads due to a fear of being hijacked by Dan; when he came to a road, having skulked there via hedges, he dashed across and threw himself behind cover. His moves were impeded by tools and building materials, and to see him rush between caravans whilst holding a length of drain pipe was like seeing an infantryman going into action with a mortar.

He also wore disguises; a beard, floppy hat or voluminous coat, which made him stand out in a crowd and which even drew J. C.'s half-baked attention.

Things came to a head with the robbery.

Hervé, making his way through a hedge, came across a couple of campers. Estranged by the vacation from their television on which they were wont to watch detective stories, they were quietly reading thrillers when Hervé popped up.

"Don't shoot," cried the husband, observing the heavy duty Black and Decker that Hervé carried, "take what you want and don't drill us."

And so saying, he and his wife stripped off their jewellery and forced it into Hervé's surprised hands.

Being an honest citizen where everything except women was concerned, he toted the lot to reception where he explained to J. C. that he had discovered it in the toilet.

And so when the campers arrived and found that the gents watch, ladies watch, cufflinks, bracelet and necklace had been recovered, they pressed a reward into his hand.

And failed to recognise him as he was wearing a bulbous nose with prominent veins and a straggly grey beard, instead of the black eye patch and droopy moustache that he had used when mistaken for a footpad.

And due to pressure from J.C. who did not want the campsite to come under scrutiny, and Hervé whose beard was working loose, and the victims themselves who had read what the underworld did to informers who grassed, the matter was not reported to the police but it did make J. C. begin to wonder.

"Why do you wear strange clothes and change your face?" he asked as Hervé pushed pads into his cheeks prior to venturing out in public. And Hervé had to confess that it was because of Dan who wished to change his appearance without resorting to props.

A Courier's Reports are Never...

"I will speak to him." said J. C., annoyed at the amount of time wasted by Hervé taking circuitous routes and applying disguises, and as I passed he was doing so at top volume.

"You can't ban me." snarled Dan, seeing his favourite diversion going up the spout.

Madam S trotted out of reception to see what the noise was.

"I can. It's my site." yelled J.C., and Madam blinked at this premature appropriation of the inheritance.

"Like hell," snapped Dan, being on firm ground, "it's your daddy's."

Although he had never seen one, J.C. gave a passable imitation of an Irish jig.

"You're banned," he screamed, "do not come on this site again."

Madam S gulped and flapped her mouth about. Dan thrust his whiskers close to J.C.'s brick-red face.

"If I go, sonny," he said, "I withdraw all our mobiles.

"No" wailed Madam S, at the thought of the income from 34 mobiles disappearing down the road hitched to Dan's van.

And inserting herself between the antagonists she pushed a surprised, steaming J. C. backwards into reception.

"It's just his sense of humour," she called gaily over her shoulder, "of course you're always welcome here."

I continued on towards the phone as J.C.s heel caught on the step and he disappeared backwards together with a stand full of pretty picture postcards.

Strange, I mused, how pride comes before a fall.

- O -

"I'm phoning Rupert about Jean-Crapface," growled Winston, "the bastard had a go at Minnie."

"Sexually?" I exclaimed, as this was uppermost in my mind due to my early morning workouts being punctuated by heavy breathing from Edith's mobile. It seemed that she and Hervé were exercising along with me but making much harder work of it.

"He gave her a dressing down."

"Dressing or undressing?" I said, still on one track.

He looked at me oddly then explained how J. C. had called Minnie to reception, ranted at her for telling Rupert that the restaurant had closed, and said that she was not to inform her office of anything that happened on the site. Which seemed a good enough reason for me to put it in my weekly report.

Then I pottered into reception to view the great man's mood for myself. Personal experience gives of a more factual writing.

"I want to see you in the gym." he said abruptly.

"Gloves, swords or pistols?" I asked.

He stopped short. "Er, immediately." he said.

So we repaired to the gym, closely followed by Madam S and her husband, who had hurried over when informed that their son was having half a brainstorm and she may need help in tying him down.

We found that the gym was also in need of repair. The weights were strewn around, the bars had been used to jab holes in the ceiling, the rowing machine was broken and games had been thrown onto the floor.

"Look at this mess." J.C. cried, crunching about and making it worse. He waived his arms, kicked at a weight, hopped about shouting 'ouch' and spread his arms dramatically. "It is the English who did this?

Mother stepped forward in a worried way but I forestalled her.

"Did Jacques teach them French?" I asked, pointing to filthy

phrases written in his language on the mirror. "Even the drawings are not in English."

"Ah" he said, peering at sketches of genitalia.

"And this word on the table in spray paint is not Anglo– Saxon."

Mother turned her eyes away and inflamed her cheeks.

"Oh." said J.C.

"English crudities are far more sophisticated," I told them, "which reminds me, why is the restaurant closed?"

Mother gasped, father shuddered, J.C. went red as he built up a head of steam and I stepped close and blandly smiled into his face.

With a gentle whistling sound his chest deflated.

"Er. It was not making much, very few customers." he explained.

"A good reason to close it," I said, "but I hope you will keep the takeaway open. It is very popular."

"Yes, it makes money." he said, showing his instinct for business; which again jogged my memory.

"The toilets smell" I said.

He called over a man who was standing in the corner wearing horn-rimmed glasses with no lens and a blond afro wig.

"Will you clean out the cess pit, Hervé?" he asked.

And I strolled off thinking what a nice obliging chap J.C. was.

Your courier always finds the bright side.

- O -

We brightened our evening with a visit to Winston.

Edith was also invited and as we sat around chewing nuts, crisps, jellied frogs legs, and drinking wine, the door suddenly opened and a man strode in.

Pushing the bowls of nosh to the far end and tipping Edith's glass down her, he spread a map on the table and spoke to Winston.

"'ere, Winnie," he said, "what's the best way to Cherbourg?"

"Don't call me Winnie" said Winston, "and can't you see we're eating?"

"You're not." said the man, quite correctly as we had stopped partly due to his map covering the bowls and partly due to surprise.

"Piss off." suggested Winston.

"I'm going to," said the man, quite unmoved, "but very early in the morning and I want to be sure of the route."

"Go to Rennes," said Winston, "and turn right. That's the best way; through St. Nazaire."

"Really" said the man, surprised.

"Better roads" replied Winston, "you'll do it in three hours."

"Gee thanks," Winnie," said the man, "I'm glad I asked."

"Winston." said Winston.

"By the way, Winnie," he said, folding the map and moving to the door, "will the barrier be down at 6 a.m.?"

"No," said Winston, "they raise it at 5.30."

"O K, thanks," said the man, "have a good evening."

As he left Edith appeared from the kitchen where she was sponging her dress. "St. Nazaire," she said, "is about 60 miles south of Rennes, and the most direct route to

A Courier's Reports are Never…

Cherbourg takes six hours."

"Does it really," said Winston, "that slipped my memory."

"And," added Sandy, "the barrier goes up at seven."

"Not to worry," said Winston complacently, "he'll find out for himself."

And he poured another glass of wine, courtesy of Heavenly Holidays, and sat back to enjoy the evening.

But not for long.

"It's probably that bloke coming back." said Sandy as a knock sounded.

But it was a different person to whom Minnie opened the door.

This one had protruding teeth and large red ears that supported a straw boater. And, stepping into the mobile, he hiccupped, looked at Edith, and spoke.

"Eet is lonely wizout you."

"Hervé." she cried.

"Bloody hell," said Sandy, "what does he want?"

That was obvious as he sat next to Edith and placed a hand on her knee. But she leapt up with a merry cry and grabbed a bottle.

"Have some wine." she said, pouring him a glass.

"Don't give that creature our wine." said Sandy.

"I look everywhere." continued Hervé, morosely emptying the glass.

"Go and look some more." said Sandy.

"I look in ze mobile, in our bed. . . ."

"More wine." sang Edith, gaily pouring.

"Our bed?" asked Sandy.

"Edith and me." replied Hervé, removing the stage teeth so as to drink faster.

"I thought you love Elulia." said Sandy.

"I do but she is gone."

"But she will come back."

"Until zen," said Hervé, scratching an ear moodily and looking surprised when it came off, "I am lonely so I fuck Edith."

"Oh my, is that the time?" cried Edith.

A Courier's Reports are Never...

"What a lovely fellow you are." said Sandy sarcastically.

"Zank you," said Hervé, "and it is good that I practice the fuck."

"Oh gosh! I have to phone my daughter." exclaimed Edith, dashing outdoors.

"Take this creature with you." called Sandy, but Edith was gone.

Hervé glumly dropped his teeth and ears into his hat as Minnie watched with horrified fascination, then spoke.

"She 'as gone again. I look everywhere for her…"

"Oh, knock it off, Herve" said Winston.

"But Zat is what I do." he cried.

I decided to edit this scene from my weekly report.

What the Office doesn't know, the Boss doesn't grieve over.

- O -

SMARTCAMP HOLIDAYS

Couriers Weekly Report

Site Name: St. Armand   Report N°: 14

Couriers: Peter and Sandy

Week Ending: 28th August

(Summarise your week including details of Weather, Site and Client Problems, Facilities and Competition)

A star hovers over the campsite. But, it is not, as the Bethlehem star, to attract, but rather, as the star of Armageddon, to repel. It is called J-C Superstar, and he has almost reached the Zenith of his ire. French Heavenly campers phoned their French office and complained that the restaurant closed on Sunday the 23rd. (The closure was a unilateral action by J–C Super-clown because most French independent campers had left by the 20th and, in accordance with site policy, he refrained from informing the companies) So Heavenly France phoned for little Minnie Heavenly-Courier to enquire if this were true and, whilst waiting for her to come to the phone, chatted to the reception girl. This girl is to finish next weekend so, feeling herself indispensible to the running of the campsite, she told them that all facilities would close at the month's end.

The wild, passionate Heavenly France phoned this info through to Heavenly England who phoned Mucus for confirmation, then phoned J-C Super-clod to say he couldn't do it. Mucus checked their contract, phoned J-C Super-twit, and told him to retain all facilities until end-Sept. J-C Super-brat, then called Minnie Heavenly to the Office and raved at her for ten minutes, reducing her to a mass of sobbing jelly, so her boyfriend phoned Heavenly England to complain and they contacted J-C Super-oaf and informed him that he was not to speak to their couriers in such a manner, that the comments had come from his office girl anyway, and he must immediately apologise to Minnie. As his vocabulary does not include words of apology, his mother had to do this on his behalf.

And so he sheds sweetness and light all around. I popped into reception to see him, to confront him about facilities. 'I want to see you in the gym,' said Super-mouth, 'it has been vandalised.' So we went and looked at the scrabble game thrown on the floor, the playing cards littering the tables, and the words scrawled in French on the walls. 'It is not the English who did this; I told him, 'they are professionals and would have made a thorough job.' And when he had stopped waving his arms and striding about to the consternation of his watching parents who now know that they should have slapped him when he was smaller, I asked why the restaurant was closed and if he would have the smell eliminated from the toilets near our tents. That slowed him down.

The restaurant is closed due to lack of patronage and he will have the toilets fixed immediately.

Mr. Clog wanted to be in Benemaas but we were all he could get. I explained that this availability was due to clients cancelling on hearing that Sandy and I were the couriers. He went back to tent 2 and chatted to his new friend Mr.Gobbi who also wanted a more hectic holiday and their ensuing antics made them the subject of a special report.

Once more, on the premise that doctors are lacking in hygiene, I put, Dr.Drip into tent eleven next to the toilets. Then found that he was a research chemist and his doctorate was not medicinal. In fact he was researching pollution and we spent happy moments discussing exhaust emission levels as I tried to take his mind off the abluting campers nearby. But my concern was misplaced. Next day I found him cheerfully taking a doctor's holiday by measuring the emission of uric acid crystals generated by a urinating Frenchman at a distance of fifteen feet as indicated by mini-litres in volumes of air, or some such.

Our quote of the week was made by a Mucus client, who dashed up to their courier shouting, 'quick, do you have a blood pressure monitor? I want to take my mother's level while she's having an attack.' I don't think that even our clients could equal that. But it might be an idea to put a surgeon's do-it-yourself kit in the Treasure Chest.

Chapter 20

Grievous bodily harm took on a new meaning as she hovered in a hostile manner in reception entrance. Of enormous bell-shaped proportions, it grieved me to see the harm that gluttony could do to what was originally a human body.

A Courier's Reports are Never...

Percy-phone Skids, our off-season cheap offer, had arrived.

"I gorra bone ter pick wi' you." she announced.

It was a changeable week for both weather and dispositions.

The previous day had brought sunshine and the sunny nature of Mr. Mucus. Not the Marvin Mucus who had succumbed to the mature charm of Edith, but a Martin Mucus who had succumbed to the manured chores of a market garden. A horticulturist was he, and therefore a fitting candidate for tent eleven.

He arrived after we had given up and gone to bed. And, seeing a light in Edith's mobile and hearing the sound of movement therein, he hammered on her door with a cry of, "I say, you in there?"

Unfortunately the sounds were caused by the fornicating Hervé who had Edith jammed exhaustedly against the stove. And being somewhat preoccupied when the hammering broke out, he thought the voice shouted, "Hervé, you in there?" Also he suffered from an understandably well developed persecution complex and an inability to distinguish one English voice from the next. So, as Edith tottered along to answer the door, he threw the potted fern through the rear window and leapt after it.

Mr. Mucus was somewhat surprised to have the door opened by a dishevelled naked lady to the sound of smashing glass, rather like the dramatic appearance of a pantomime witch, but being an English gentleman he made no mention, merely tipped his hat and said, 'I'm Mr. Mucus.'

"You're with Smartcamp." replied Edith, for I had told her so.

"I know," replied Mucus, "but I thought it such a co-incidence, our names you know, that I just had to tell you."

Wordlessly Edith pointed towards where I, having been roused by the sounds of breaking glass, tearing cloth, muffled curses and running footsteps, was stepping forth from our camper.

"Smartcamp?" called Mr. Mucus, striding up, hand outstretched, "what an unusual site you have here."

Or perhaps he said 'sight`. I may have misheard.

- O -

And next day, as previously mentioned, this unbelievable sight appeared.

"Bone?" I said, "as in stew."

"Bone, as in contention." Percy-Phone replied, showing an unexpected spurt of erudition.

A Courier's Reports are Never...

It seemed that four of the children she intended to bring, decided at the last minute that they would rather stay with their mothers; a preference I could fully understand. So, with one day's notice, she tried to cancel the second tent, but was turned down.

"I want me money back." she said.

I explained that the financial side of Smartcamp was not handled by me.

"They'll 'ear more o' this." she declared.

I said I was sure they would, that they enjoyed corresponding with clients, and offered the address of Head Office.

"This kind a thing's a drain on Social Services," she said, "makin' 'em pay when they shouldn't." I said nothing; being rendered thoughtful.

The DAILY NEWS

Monday 4th September 1992   20p

PRISON PRIVATISATION

The Government is asking private companies to tender for management of various prisons in England, a report issued today stated. If the contract is issued to other than the Prison Service, Strangeways would be the first to be independently run.

A spokesman for the tenderer most likely to be accepted commented. 'We at Smartcamp have had vast experience in this field, mainly in France where the use of the guillotine and the rack is encouraged. Our camps are amongst the most secure in the world and our inmates the most brainwashed.'

When asked if present facilities would be modernised he stated, 'Our camps have all modern facilities including slopping out times, de-lousing showers, soup kitchens and exercise yards where activity couriers torture people with calisthenics, bingo and quizzes.'

When asked if this was not against recommended human rights he replied. 'Our punters sign away all rights when they book so that`s their problem'.

Questioned on the subject of security he quoted several instances of mutiny by clients.

'But our couriers are trained to subdue any human traits punters may exhibit,' he said, 'They are given a free hand and some of them have very strange ways.'

Typical Smartcamp entrance.

A Courier's Reports are Never...

"De're proivitoisin prisons." said a voice from outside and Mrs. Skids flowed out to join a small thin, puffy-faced man who was propped against my notice board with his head at a dislocated angle as he read it.

"Dat's a good ting," he opinioned, "dey got no comfort where's da bar?"

"Pardon?" I said.

"Where's da bar oi got dis dreadful turst?" he replied and I realised that he always spoke in one continuous sentence.

"We'll git a kids inna tent first." declared Percy-phone, and after skirmishing with me about the kids club activities, she put her leprechaun into the car and I took them to their tents.

"What a strange name." said Sandy, reading the police fitch Mrs. Skids had made out and mispronouncing Persephone.

So Percy—phone she became and we often saw her lumbering along as she made her way to the pool, leaving her leprechaun in the bar. And whenever she squeezed her way through the gateway in the fence around the pool, other bathers would flee, leaving her in solitary possession. She would lurch around the enclosure in her white swimsuit, looking like a polar bear in a pit, and, although no one threw nuts and fruit to her, I felt that the Social Services were getting their money's worth.

And we slipped off to run a Kids Club while her cubs weren't looking.

- O -

Our Kids Club ploy had been foiled by a Head Office directive informing all sites that only reasonable pursuits were to be pursued. Possibly some unscrupulous couriers had been manipulating the activities to suit their own ends and, although I could see their point, one had to do one's best for the nippers. And knowing that they always enjoyed digging for cockles and watching us eat them, we advertised a preponderance of healthy outdoor pastimes. And so Kids Club should have been easy. But, after the advent of Pine and Green, it wasn't.

We waited up for them as usual, and when they failed to arrive as usual, we went to bed as usual. But as I made my pre-dawn check on the mobiles' gas cylinders, I noticed that the tents reserved for them were occupied, which was unusual.

A quick glance at the planner sheet disclosed no record of their arrival and Sandy's "who, what" showed that she had not billeted them whilst I slept. Perhaps Edith had let them in, but from sounds in her mobile I knew she was occupied and not available for questioning, and Winston's temperament precluded his giving assistance to clients, even when not his own. It was baffling.

Until Mr. Pine explained that as a former courier he knew the system and had billeted the party. So we took their kids gratefully under our wings, and then wished we hadn't.

Mother Pine pressed her little daughter's hand into mine and prized her own free. Then walked off as the kid yelled and swung bonelessly round in my grip like a screaming top.

Father Pine brought her to the next meeting where she went through the same routine with Sandy; and all the way to the beach and back people looked accusingly at us as though we were child abusers, which I wished we were.

And so, in spite of the club providing us with free labour to collect our cockles, we decided that enough was too much, cancelled further meetings and put up a notice about child abuse to deter parents. And set about arranging something for ourselves.

- O -

CHILDRENS COURIERS WEEKLY REPORT

Site Name: St.Quentin Penitentiary   Date: 4th September
Couriers: Jack the Ripper and Ma.Brady   Numbers: would prefer one less

Venue on Site: Exercise Yard

Advertised Programme: Saturday; Beach Ramble. Monday; Beach Hunt. Wednesday; Beach Party. Friday; Beach Games.

General Summary of Week: Saturday; took kids for a ramble along the estuary; showed them trees and leaves and told them what type they were which was probably wrong, but the nine kids didn't know any better.

Monday, Wednesday and Friday; in every instance we were overruled by the kids who wanted to go cockling; crabbing not having been discovered by this lot.

Any incidents or comments

Little Sophie Pine screamed during the whole of Wednesday and Friday club meets which led to accusations and allegations from onlookers but Sandy should be released from police custody by Monday, subject to good behaviour, which will be in time for her to bid the child farewell.

The DAILY NEWS

Monday 6th September 1992   20p

ABUSE

An allegation that Smartcamp couriers were using hypnosis on their charges at Children's Club was made today by the R.S.P.C.C.

'We found the children huddled together in a corner of the Children's Tent at St.Armand, eyes glazed watching a swinging metal disk while the couriers drank and smoked and occasionally lashed them with a whip; stated one horrified official,

'Yet after the meeting the children said that they had enjoyed playing games and eating pancakes.

In his reply Fred Smart-Camp, the firms' owner, commented, 'it is up to the individual courier how he runs the club and keeps the little rotters under control. I reckon these couriers showed initiative and the little swine's weren`t harmed permanent were they?'

He then recounted how one courier had chained his children to trees for two hours and another had locked them in a car. 'You pays your money and you takes your pick,' he said with a laugh. Meanwhile the R.S.P.C.C. has recommended that children should be kept away from the club.

'One just doesn`t know what diabolical tricks they will think up next,' said a spokesman.

Some Childrens Club members yesterday.

170

A Courier's Reports are Never...

Having experienced hospitality from Edith in her pre-Hervé period, and having a long standing invite to join her in a birthday lunch next week, we decided to reciprocate and have her for a meal.

But as we drove off to shop and I paused to remind her of this and Sandy interjected, "don't bring that creature," she made excuses which caused us to ponder as we drove to the supermarket, and think deeply as we returned. And Sandy asked me to write a letter to Elulia, so I wrote the following:

Dear Elulia,

I am writing about this at the behest of Big Sand as we both feel that it is peculiar and you will find it more interesting than somewhat.

We is leaving the camp to shop when we sees Edith out for a stroll with an Alsatian of your acquaintance and so we stop and I address her as follows: "Hello Edith, we is off to the Hyper for grub for tonight's nosh of which I wish to remind you." "Oh gosh," she says, "I is more than sorry to inform you that I cannot make our date as my only sister's daughter has given birth to a bouncing none year old this very instant, and I must dash over and wet the baby's head as she, my only sister, is over the moon with delight and nothing will deter her from insisting that we celebrate this big event this evening.

"That is very nice," we says, "for all and sundry and we hope you will extend out felicitations to your only sister on this momentous occasion and if we can help in any way feel free to ask."

"There is one thing," she replies, "and that is if you can purchase for me a phone card so that I can let all our family and friends know of this great event." She ponders for a moment and continues, "it would be best if you get the larger card for 100 francs as I tend to run off at the mouth and the smaller card Will not allow of this."

"Right, Edith," we say, "we will do as you ask and are glad that your sister is happy."

"Over the moon" repeats Edith, "as this is her first grandchild and I am sorry to break our date but you can see how it is." "It is surely understandable and quite acceptable." we say, and with that continue to the Hyper after first calling at the post office for a phone card.

I am deliberating between a vin de l'Aude and a Côte du Rhone when Sandy approaches from the direction of the fruit counter and, looking thoughtful, speaks thus, "guess who I ran into."

Now I am into the serious business of selecting wine and in no mood for trivial guessing games so I suggest various persons from Santa Claus to Robin Hood but Sandy stamps her foot in an irritated manner and says, "Sue."

I am aware of a dozen Sues of our acquaintance and point this out, but she stamps her foot again and clarifies her statement.

"Sue, stupid," she says, "of the Sue and Sid duet." "Edith's only sister," I reply enlightened, "then I hope that you conveys at first hand our congratulations on becoming a granny."

"That is just the point," she says, "for she knows nothing of the birth."

"She is over the moon," I suggest, "and perhaps not yet come down."

"No," responds Big Sand thoughtfully, "for her statement that issue is not yet produced was seconded by Sid in no uncertain terms as is his wont."

"This is most baffling," I say, baffled, "and I cannot deduce the answer."

"Unless," says Big Sand, clicking her fingers, "she is looking for an excuse to avoid our company."

And, agreeing with Sand who is usually right in these things, I drive back to camp.

"Hi there, Edith," I call, "we has got the phone card to enable you to inform all and sundry that you are now an aunt."

"Thank you," she says, "I will commence this instant."

"What did the baby weigh?" asks Big Sand, who is well versed in these things.

"Seven and a half pounds," replies Edith promptly, "which is about right for a little girl."

"Do not forget to congratulate your only sister." Big Sand reminds her, and with a, "most certainly." Edith hurries off towards the phone box.

"How will she get out of this one?" asks Big Sand.

"She will wriggle," I reply, "and say the office misinformed her. Or is it only snakes that wriggle?"

- O -

SMARTCAMP HOLIDAYS

Couriers Weekly Report

Site Name: st. Armand   Report N°: 15

Couriers: Peter and sandy

Week Ending: 4th September

(Summarise your week including details of Weather, Site and Client Problems, Facilities and Competitors)

A Courier's Reports are Never...

I noticed that we were to have a Mr. Mucus to stay, so told the Mucus courier that he was the owner of her firm, travelling with us to find out, what comfort meant. She met him before we did. We waited up until midnight then crawled into bed. He arrived at 1 a.m. and hammered on the door of Mucus reception mobile. Edith dragged her tired self to the door from where she was slumped between the table and the stove, and looked at him. 'Hello; he said brightly, 'I'm Mr. Mucus'. 'You're with Smart camp, she replied. 'I know; he said. She pointed him our way and went back to her coma.

As he is a horticulturist, and used to fertilizer, we put him in tent number eleven which Dr. Drip had vacated in favour of a mobile. "Conveniences are convenient." I said busily hoodwinking. "By Jove yes," he replied, "not far to go, darling." The latter was addressed to his wife, a permed middle aged, well bred lady, and not to me. Next day I saw her and her mother taking tea, with little fingers raised, sitting contentedly with their backs to a row of urinating campers. Some English people still have aplomb.

Our next arrival was totally lacking in aplomb.

Persephone Skids is remarkably fat, and shaped like a bell. When she turns suddenly, her flesh hesitates then follows her round rather like the flow of a reluctant amoeba. A difficult person she needs a special report all to herself. The other clients, although strong enough to brave most inclement elements, took one look and decided to leave a day early. They left oddments which we offered to Percy-phone. She took the bottle of water but declined the washing up liquid and spray cleaner. "Wot we wont wi at?" she demanded, "we aint doin no cleanin." Oh for the halcyon days of Unutterably Foul or Stonewall Jackson.

The people who left, Siddons and Wight, were travelling together and disproved the theory that couples exclude other campers. A nice friendly gregarious lot, they mixed with and organised things in the Smartcamp enclave where we joined them of an evening. It was fortunate they were there as we couldn't arrange a get together due to changeable weather. So we had impromptu events, with all the tables and brollies in a row like a street party, until the advent of the malign Percy-phone.

The next dual travellers were Pine end Green. These were friends as opposed to Siddons and Wight being relatives, and mixed only with each other. We waited up for them until 2 a.m. then retired. Next morning they were sound asleep in their tents. They had arrived at 2.30 a.m. and, unlike the usual nocturnal Smartcamp traveller who slams on our door with the beguiling cry of, "come out and earn your money," they had crept into reception, noted their tent numbers, found the tents and dossed themselves down. We gave them a big thank you and that Children's Club sticker of the Bear painting glue on his mouth.

Madam S has always been courteous to me, on occasions does not speak to Sandy, tends to ignore the Mucus courier, and she and her son J. C. sneer at, and throw stones at, the Heavenly couriers. All in all, I suppose, fairly normal behaviour for campsite owners.

Quote of the week was from a car-load of Mucus clients who screamed off shouting, "we're going; we're leaving this dustbin." The dustbin they referred to must have been their mobile which they left in such a state that it may never recover.

CHAPTER 21

As with Edith, the season wriggled and undulated its way to an end. But did it slowly and painfully like a snake shedding its skin.

Clients were leaving in dribbles and drabbles in accordance with our programme and, as they left, we packed the equipment in the tents ready for the montage team to stow into more permanent accommodation on the site, or return to the stores for repair or replacement.

Mr. Mucus took his ladies off to fields of a different aroma.

Percy-phone wrangled about repayment, children's club and the sudden blast of sunny weather. As she had more skin than most, I suppose that sunburn was more painful for her.

SmartCamp Notice:

CHILDRENS CLUB

End of Seasons Specials:

Monday:

Body Dissecting at Benemaas Mortuary.

Wednesday:

Upside down One Foot Hang Gliding over Point du Raz

Thursday:

Breath Holding Competition in Oceanopolis shark tank.

Saturday:

Chicken Run. Who can slap a sticker on the fastest car on Quimper Motorway.

Sunday:

Church Dedication Service for recently departed members.

A Courier's Reports are Never...

I had put up a special children's club notice but it failed to entice the Skid's charges and the only comment came from her leprechaun who said:"Dem's unusual activities but interestin and drink is expensive in dis place."

And then she abruptly left to the sound of threats and a labouring engine and the sun shone more brightly without her to impede it.

We continued to minister to our diminishing clientele and winterise the mobiles as they deserted them.

_Winston continued to desert his clientele and diminish and chill them with his lack of ministrations.

It was about 6.30 in the morning when one of his clients, unable to rouse him from slumber, set about changing his own gas cylinder, being sorely in need of breakfast.

But, unable to connect the new one, he returned to Winston's sanctuary, knocked on the door for a while, began to emote frustrated anger, eventually picked up the empty cylinder and smashed it repeatedly against the dented side Of the mobile.

Until the bedroom window shattered and the panting client found Winston regarding him through the empty frame.

"Hang about," said Winston, "I want to see if you've paid the damage waiver."

He seemed to have a way with clients.

- O -

SPECIAL REPORT

Site: St. Armand   Date: 9th September
Couriers: Peter and Sandy

Clients Name: Percephone Skids

(Detail the complaint/problem and action taken)

Percy-phone Skids is a large, pear-shaped ungainly creature that lumbers on flat feet, and who can blame them. Her entourage consists of a small bucolic drunken Irishman and three distorted children. "The other four bleeders wouldn't come at the last minute," she said, explaining the discrepancy in the booking, "they're staying with their mothers." Percy-phone fosters kids by profession and is probably here by courtesy of the Social Services. "Kids wouldn't come, I tried to cancel the other tent but Smartcamp wouldn't give me a penny back." she snarled, her mouth wrinkling like the underside of a barnacle.

She asked what site activities there were for the children. I told her these had just finished but we held children's club meetings. This made her snort but she never sent the kids to us and stated that we held no certificate of competence from a recognised body. "Bleeding amateurs." She described us.

So after the final meeting of the season I put up a notice headed 'abuse' to prove her point.

On the 5th I called on Percy-phone to say that only one of her tents had been extended for the extra two days she had booked as she left home, but as we had a spare tent, the kids could remain in the second tent. "I wouldn't move anyway," she said belligerently, "I paid a lotta loot fa this oliday" Her Irish consort roused at the tone of voice and peered at me over his breakfast. "Dere's a lot of child abuse on dis campsite," he said, "I read it on your board." "The French is disgusting," said Percy-phone, "this abuse wouldn't appen in England." "It's a joke for the children." I said. "Then it's not really true?" asked Percy-phone, looking slightly mollified, "just a joke, eh?" "It still shouldn't be allowed." said the Irishman, pouring more wine on his cornflakes, "it's a disgusting way to behave."

Action taken: As far as possible I treated her as though she was human, but she may have been disconcerted by my habit of only talking to her whilst regarding her reflection in a mirror so as not to be turned to stone.

The state of her tents on leaving was unhygienic and the children's tent smelt as though something had crawled in there and died. However I was fascinated by her sleeping habits. Ingenious campers rearrange the beds to suit themselves, e.g. putting the double bed into the large inner or turning the single bed sideways, but she was the best yet. She put the two single beds side by side complete with mattresses and placed the double mattress on top. Her little Irish friend slept on the double bed frame, unprotected from its springs; but in his state I doubt that he would notice.

- O -

The morning of Edith's birthday dawned clear, sunny and mild. And so she put tables on a nearby empty plot, covered them with Mucus blankets and set places for us all.

Sid and Sue were at the far end together with Edith and Hervé. Sandy and I at the opposite end, Winston and Winnie and our friends Bill and Fiona were seated in the middle; thereby illustrating how Edith had distanced herself from us ever since the abortive birth.

Bill and Fiona were visiting now that our work had quietened down and the site on which they worked had finished. "It's been another awfully dull summer," said Fiona, "Nothing much ever happens." said Bill; thus demonstrating that they could do a courier's job with their eyes closed. But then, they had been at it for a number of years.

"Will you be a courier again next year?" asked Fiona.

"Yeah," said Winston, "we might as well. There's nothing to it."

I suppose that depends on how you approach the job.

And as we sat chewing and chatting, nemesis was approaching; but of this we were blithely unaware.

Having read a newspaper report about the much hounded Princess of Wales, I had written a notice based on it, but featuring Edith, entitled Edith-gate. Which could have been why she was flickering glances in our direction although it, did not explain why Hervé was flickering glances towards the entrance gate.

Unable to wear shoes, Hervé had been limping painfully about with bandaged feet encased in carpet slippers. He had cut his feet on broken window glass and they were obviously sore. Edith seemed unable to sit for very long and was constantly leaping up to refuel the barbecue, pass serviettes, or wait on Hervé. We sat and drank and ambled across to the fire every now and then to turn the meat we had brought and char the other side.

A standard relaxed lunchtime was therefore in progress with sunshine filtering through trees and competing with the Mucus blankets, birds atwittering in the background, barbecue smoking, meat spoiling, people shifting, scratching, laughing, drinking and engaging in vapid conversation. All in all the kind of scene that is photographed for a brochure to encourage envious workers to spend their hard earned on trying to purchase an illusion.

The DAILY NEWS

Monday 11th September 1992   20p

EDITHGATE

Confidential sources have revealed that senior protection officers from Scotland Yard were secretly summoned to Horse Muck Palace, the home of Lord Mucus, to be questioned about the movements of the Duchess of Edithborough.

Mucus apparently expressed concern that on six occasions Edith dispensed with her personal protection officer and went alone to appointments. On those occasions she switched off her beeper and deactivated monitoring equipment inside her car.

'This service is for protection,' Mucus emphasised,' and there is no intention of infringing on her personal liberties.'

However friends point out that she has no appointments after October and this has fuelled rumours of a split.
Also MI5 have tapped an Edithgate type telephone conversation with an un-known man.

'It was very personal,' commented a detective, 'And the man addressed her as Squeegee.'

A telephone that might be similar to the one used by the Duchess when she was tapped by MI5.

These revelations could seriously undermine the Mucus hierarchy and affect future relations.

'We do not know who the man is,' stated a Special Branch Officer, 'But we are very worried for his safety.'

A Courier's Reports are Never...

I drifted across to where Sid was prodding an unidentifiable piece of charred something on the barbecue and coughing gently in the smoke.

"Nice girl sometimes is Edith," he opinioned, being magnanimous because it was her birthday, "good of her to invite that Hervé bloke."

"Big hearted," I agreed.

"Very generous at times. Give people anything."

"Or everything."

"Yes," he said, making me wonder, "what she's got she spreads around."

"I'm sure."

"Take that French bloke there. Not the sort of person anyone in their right mind would bother with. But she looks after him."

I had to agree. We watched her wipe at stains on his newly ironed shirt, and hand him a knife and fork.

"Waits on him hand and foot." said Sid.

Again I agreed, knowing that she had bathed and bandaged his feet.

"Yes," said Sid charitably, as he scraped his smouldering something across the blackened sooty grill, "I wouldn't think many people want him."

And suddenly, as though to disprove his words, nemesis struck.

The still, balmy air was rent by the sounds of breaking branches as Dan smashed his way through the hedge behind Hervé.

The latter gave off a frightened squeal and sprang upright on his bandages, then rushed round the table in hopping leaps with Dan in close pursuit.

Under normal circumstances Hervé would have shown Dan a clean pair of heals instead of the neatly bound ones he now displayed. He would have done his startled rabbit, impersonation and been at the door to his burrow, which we could see up the road beyond the workshop before Dan could say 'Jaques Rouge-gorge—fils`.

Had a professional handicapper been present he would have pursed his lips and muttered "too much," and a professional bookmaker would have given odds on in favour of Dan.

So Hervé turned the race into a steeplechase by capering round the tables and casting empty chairs, sunshades and bowls of salad into Dan's path, causing him to stumble about and shout oaths about fair play. And as they careered around filling the air with yells, screams, the sound of smashing dishes and of breaking chairs, I looked to see how the others were taking it.

Edith ignored her lover's plight by bending over her plate and studiously eating. Sue and Sid, also being employed by Dan and therefore not impartial, carried on with whatever they were doing. Winston, to whom displays of anger on the campsite were commonplace, noticed nothing unusual and continued chewing, and Minnie, as always, followed his lead.

Bill and Fiona stopped eating and sat, mouths open and eyes popping, watching the action. And Sandy, who felt that Hervé had dished the dirt on her friend Elulia and it would be best if he were removed from her life, continued chatting.

"Will you work as couriers again next year?" she asked Bill.

"Yes." he replied absently, flinching at a particularly violent thrust Dan made at Hervé with a barbecue fork, "we rather enjoy the tranquil atmosphere of a campsite."

"So do we," said Sandy, "and it's so much quieter with fewer clients."

"Yeah," agreed Winston, as Hervé rushed past, snatched up a broken branch from the hedge and deftly thrust it between Dan's legs, "it's more peaceful when the bastards have gone."

Dan screamed as he fell against the barbecue and the hot coals cascaded down his leg, and Hervé took the opportunity to break off and dash down the home straight.

He almost made it.

As Sid righted the barbecue and poured wine on the flaming grass thereabouts, Hervé threw open his door and rushed inside. But was unable to close it on Dan, who jerked it from his grasp and followed him in.

There was a pause of a few seconds while Sid searched for his charred portion and Sue picked up trampled salad, then Dan reappeared with a limp Hervé over his shoulder and carted him into the workshop.

And by the time J. C. drove past, all was serine with Edith chewing thoughtfully, Sid and Sue making subdued comments to each other, Winston cheerfully drinking, Sandy talking brightly, and Bill and Fiona responding well but casting puzzled glances at the workshop from which noise and intermittent flickering lights were emanating.

J. C. nodded to me, ignored Edith and sneered at Winston. Then he stopped by the workshop, walked to the door, nodded approval at the sounds of activity from within, changed his mind, withdrew and drove off again.

And thereby missed the sight of Dan stepping forth furtively with a sack covered bundle over his shoulder and striding off into the distance.

I finished my meat in a preoccupied way wondering a) what Dan had been doing in the workshop, b) if he had done away with Hervé and c) where he was depositing the body.

A Courier's Reports are Never...

I received no clue from Dan when he returned and we introduced him to B and F. He merely shook hands and said he was pleased to meet them, declined Edith's offer of food or drink, told S and S he would see them later, and went away in high spirits.

He didn't act like a murderer and his comment to me which was, "I couldn't do it, at the last moment. I couldn't do it." was puzzling.

So I ate my desert in a meditative manner, chewed at fruit in a wondering way, noshed cheese and biscuits with building bewilderment and then, overcome by curiosity, I went to find the remains.

I came across no newly turned soil, no freshly replaced turf.

Thickets and bramble-beds were Hervé-less and the toilets yielded not a bloodstain. I searched high, low, and in between but found naught.

Until I came to the tennis courts.

Hervé was stripped naked except for what appeared to be a tight fitting metal birdcage.

Flat iron hoops were welded round his body, arms and legs and they, in turn, were welded to each other. With arms pinioned to his sides he swung gently in the tennis court doorway, suspended by a hook at the back of the chest band.

"Fetch Edith." he croaked.

"If you insist." I said, "but at your own risk. She may be into bondage."

I went to find her wondering if, after a season of reading my notices, she would believe my description of Hervé`s plight.

People don't always believe a courier's reports.

END

Also by Peter Goodlad

Available from Amazon.

37552953R00103

Printed in Great Britain
by Amazon